SEARCHING FOR HOLY GROUND

by Helen Hill

To Order:

Principle Publisher
1-386-288-7169
www.PrinciplePublisher.com
reparker@principlepublisher.com

DEDICATION

This book is lovingly dedicated to my husband, Danny Hill, whose spiritual strength has given me the courage to share my life experiences with others. He erased the cloak of fears and insecurities and gave me confidence and love. He's my best friend and God's gift to me.

Together, we offer our gratitude to our special friends:
Rev. Charles and Edna Johnson (and son, Steve) for encouragement.
My brother, Mick Slider, who taught me to focus on my goal.
My sister, 'Babe' Haskey, who nagged me into writing.
My children, who depended on me as a role model.
My Christian friends, who prayerfully provided invaluable data for the book.

I must not forget to thank three precious souls:
My Publisher, Earline Parker, who walked me through my first book.
My Cover Artist, Duffy Soto, who has humility and God-given talent.
My Photographer, Michelle Jones and daughter, Kenidy, for the cover work.

This book has been a healing experience and I thank my Lord and Savior, Jesus Christ.

CHAPTERS PAGE

FOREWORD

"Trust in the Lord, and do good; so shalt thou dwell in the land, and verily thou shalt be fed." Psalm 37:3

There once was a child who sensed a Holy presence in her life at an early age. She had welcomed the Spirit of God as He led her through dysfunctional experiences. She walked with Him through dark valleys and evil principalities. In every experience, there was a lesson to be learned, a new step to take on a pathway to...?? Somehow, she knew she was on a journey.

Her goal was to spend eternity praising God, walking streets of gold, but that destination had a special charted highway that took her through amazing adventures. Little did she know in her search was the key to a treasure...Holy Land...where seekers came face to face with the miraculous works of the Omnipotent God... where the Holy Ghost dwelled among believers! This land...this Holy Land is real. These people are ready to share their life stories...miracles!

Be prepared to feast on His Word and hear the promises and covenant He has honored throughout generations. Get ready to be introduced to chosen children of God. Open your hearts and spiritual eyes for Jesus Christ is ready to greet *You!*

You might want to remove your shoes...
for soon you shall walk on Holy Ground!

Your Sister In Christ's Service,
Helen Hill

CHAPTER I

In the Beginning, God Created Possibilities!

(October 1957) The moon was full that October night and the cold autumn wind was bone chilling. I remember pushing my sister over in the bed we shared so I could wrap myself up in the old Indian blankets Mom ordered from the National Bellas Hess salesman who came selling door to door.

Snuggled in for the long cold night, I let my mind wander. In the distance, a train whistle was blowing, piercing the night air, sending a warning to clear the railroad crossing up ahead. There was something comforting in that old train whistle. It sent my mind to destinations I thought I would never reach outside of my imagination. ("O God, Thou hast taught me from my youth: and hitherto have I declared Thy wondrous works." Psalm 71:17 KJV).

It wasn't just the Norfolk and Western rolling down those tracks that stirred my heart. My dad sat outside on the front porch and smoked his pipe, listening to WWVA, Wheeling, West Virginia's 'Old Time Gospel Hour and Jubilee'. The music would drift into my bedroom in the dark and I could picture those gospel singers and musicians, their eyes closed in spiritual reverie, entertaining angels just outside heaven's pearly gates.

And then that train would come rumbling through the hills and carry me off to a new life, somewhere far away from the shanty in which we lived; someplace where love was a reality and no one cringed in fear or hid their tears and broken hearts lest they be punished even more. I wondered if God knew where I lived or did He care that love had passed us by? I wondered if Dad found peace in those late night hymns, full of promise. ("Peace I leave with you, My peace I give unto you: not as the world giveth, give I unto you. Let not your heart be troubled, neither let it be afraid." John 14:27 KJV).

Sometimes, I sneaked into the kitchen to watch Mom start her daily routine. She started a fire in the pot-bellied stove so the room would be warm for us when we got up. Then she placed the chipped blue coffee pot on top to start it perking. As she wiped her hands, I heard her start singing her favorite songs, "What A Friend We Have In Jesus" and "Rock of Ages Cleft For Me."

But as she sang those words, 'cleft for me,' her voice cracked as she fought back the tears and she stopped singing. I suppose she felt those songs that had one time brought her peace and joy were now just reminders of the overwhelming sadness with which she was dealing since she turned her back on God. ("The Lord is nigh unto them that are of a broken heart; and saveth such as be of a contrite spirit." Psalm 34:18 KJV).

I called from the doorway, "Mama, please don't stop singing," but she turned to me and scolded, "Don't you be sneakin' up on me like that. Now get on out of here!" I hung my head and walked away wishing I could hear just one more chorus from my mother's heart. Only the angels could teach her to sing like that!

What was it that kept my parents from returning to the altar (where they had been saved in the early 1940's) to repent and rededicate their lives to Jesus? I knew this was not a topic that either of them would be willing to discuss with me.

Now, I needed to know what the power was in those old time gospel songs that seemed stronger than gravity, pulling me to a hidden mystery. Soon there would be more clues, answers to questions no one else would ever hear. I had to find that Holy Ground. ("Blessed are they which do hunger and thirst after righteousness: for they shall be filled." Matt. 5:6 KJV).

CHAPTER II

Family ~ Seeds of Neglect in a Garden of Need, Lest the Master Tills the Soil

(September 27th, 1959) Dad listened to the radio again last night but it just wasn't the same as other nights. He was very angry about something but I wasn't sure what was bothering him.

It was a crazy routine at our house. Everybody either hid or left when Dad was mad. He never seemed to want to settle any arguments; he just wanted to fight. I had seen the madness in his eyes when he believed my brother, Bill, had done something to upset him.

Bill was born with a heart defect that caused Mom to fear he would die if he was not treated delicately. She often said he was pronounced dead three times but she prayed and God brought him back to her.

Dad resented weakness. He was determined to make a good strong man out of Bill but they had never bonded as father and son. Bill only related well with the boys his age who had admiration for his willingness to 'risk the consequences' to get their respect. A good laugh from the crowd was worth any discipline when he got home, but Dad reacted like a wild man, ready to swing his old army belt like a whip. I knew Bill hated him during those times. He referred to him as 'the old man.' His voice verbally rebelled, but his body crumpled like a broken, unwanted child. It brought me to tears.

I loved Bill but I don't think he ever knew it because, in our house, love was a punishable offense. He thought Dad was proud of Mickey, my oldest brother and hero, but even he was not given Dad's unconditional love. At most, it could be described as occasional acceptance.

Mickey was gifted with people around him who admired him. He was the head of his youth group at Sunday school. He respected the elderly and did chores and mowed their lawns with pride. He planned to be successful, knowing that calluses were the keys that opened doors but the maps to life's dreams were drawn with wisdom.

(Later in life, he mastered the martial arts; he opened a school, 'The Dojo,' with his son, Jason. With the blessing of God who gave him his wife [Nancy], he found a peaceful life).

He told me I could be whatever I wanted to be when I grew up. The secret was to be determined to be the best; not just until you reached your goal, but to stay the best. He also reminded me often that my competition was not from others, but my own character... me. When he enlisted in the army, to get away from our father's tyranny, I thought I had lost my best friend; even Bill seemed to get into more trouble.

To overcompensate for his inability to please his father, Bill became a comedian everywhere he went. He wanted to be a musician and tried to play the guitar like Dad. He could play a few chords and strum a little, but Dad was the first to tell him he would never amount to much because he was just too lazy to apply himself, so he quit.

He wanted to be an artist, competing with Mickey, but the one thing Bill lacked was the ability to connect with the object he drew. Mickey created beauty because he saw beauty in the eyes of the children he sketched. When he drew his pictures of Jesus, he could draw from the peace and love he had discovered at church where he got saved and felt the touch of the Master.

Bill based his efforts on jealousy, to prove he was as talented or as gifted as Mickey. I look back and wish I could tell him Jesus loved him just the way he was. He was truly gifted. He walked into a room and soon everyone was laughing because he entertained them with his funny antics.

He loved to watch the transformation he brought to a room of somber people as he lightly bantered and joked with them, and if all else failed, he would disappear and come back into the room dressed as an old hobo or as a little boy, tying his shoes around his legs at his knees and walking comically.

Once as a practical joke on his friend, on Halloween, he dressed as a sophisticated woman, (which took a lot of work). His friend was convinced he had already dated every available young woman in the county. He was a 'real lady's man,' but the strange 'lady' who knocked at his door for directions was a real challenge. After listening to all his pick- up lines, Bill couldn't take it any longer and started laughing, removing his wig.

That night, Bill tried to outrun his 'suitor' but he still came home with a black eye … and had to answer to Dad. He always knew there would be consequences for his actions, but it never stopped him from planning his next move.

His greatest talent was never wanting to say an unkind word to anyone. Each time he tried to upstage his brother, he ended up being embarrassed when he was told time after time, 'that's almost as good as Mickey's.'

I never saw him retaliate in anger. He just mumbled that it didn't matter, tossed it aside and the next time he entered the room, he would usually make a silly face to make you smile. He became a smile-giver to everyone but Dad, who was not to be pleased.

Between the two was a bridge built on distrust and neither ever ventured across to repair the damaged hearts. ("And, ye fathers, provoke not your children to wrath: but bring them up in the nurture and admonition of the Lord." Eph.6:4 KJV).

[Hindsight is perfect, for there we do everything right. Today is the time to show your love and support, for we are never promised tomorrow. An opportunity missed may be a costly mistake, for the price may be a soul guided to hell. Love restores brokenness.]

My sister was four years older and she never let me forget it. We had a friendship that probably only sisters from my background can understand. She called me names and shoved me as far out of her life as she could without feeling the wrath of Dad, choosing to be with her friends instead of saddled with a 'kid sister.' (In all fairness it must be said I was known for 'getting even' with my sister and her friends on more than one occasion, and my tactics for irritating my sister were advanced; I wrote poems about her and recited them. None, I'm afraid, were complimentary. But as combatant as we sisters were, no one was our equal when we teamed up together).

Now that I'm grown, I understand more about her rejection of me. If I had ever mentioned any of the hundreds of subjects that school girls discuss with their friends, I know now she would have been severely beaten by our father, or worse.

One thing I knew back then for sure: nobody was allowed to be mean to me when my sister was around. She protected me from bullies and even older relatives who had mean streaks about as wide as our father's. I felt safe with her, but she knew she couldn't trust me to be quiet. Nonetheless, through the years we became good friends.

But I met Someone on September 27th who became more than a Friend, for that was the day I accepted Jesus Christ who became the Navigator of my spiritual journey.

Mom had started a pot of beans cooking on the stove that morning and I smelled hot bread in the oven. I was already tasting the butter melting in my mouth from the thick slices of bread she served for our dinner.

Suddenly, I heard the door slam and the cussing started. Dad picked up the bread slicing knife and said he was going to find my brother. I didn't know what he had done, but my stomach felt like the knife had been plunged into me. Mom must have seen my face turn white because she pushed me out the door and told me to go to church and not say a word to anyone. No one knew what happened inside the four walls of our home.

There were four children in our family. No one ever went hungry or without shoes or a winter coat. That was a statement of which Mom was proud. Year after year, she wore the same ragged coat that she mended each winter, but as the winter winds began to howl, she scraped and saved to provide for her children.

She walked to work, then stood long hours at steam machines, scarring her arms at the hot presses in the commercial laundry where she worked. Her life was hard but she accepted the hard times, thankful she had a job. She rejected sympathy, and hated all the gossips and busybodies.

That day she warned me not to tell anyone we had problems, but I talked all the way to church...to God. I cried and begged and pleaded that no one would be dead when I came back home. It was a short walk to the community church but I was exhausted when I arrived. It was raining but I never felt it on my face. The tears were streaming down my cheeks and I was flushed when I dropped onto the floor of the foyer at the church. I wiped away my tears so I could see more clearly.

The pastor was downstairs in his office, but my eyes were fixed on the big picture by the coat rack. I saw Jesus in all His Glory gently cradling a little lamb. My heart was breaking as I spoke to

Him, "Jesus, could You please just hold me for a little while like that baby sheep in Your arms? I just need You today, just for a little while, ok?" That day He comforted me, became my Shepherd and He has never stopped loving me.

A child who never understood love was saved that day, and never stopped needing to find the Holy Ground where His Spirit abounds. That night the train had a gentle sound. It seemed to say, "I'm here…I'm here!" That message would lead me to miraculous destinies.

CHAPTER III

A Good Marriage Depends on Three :
A Man, A Woman, and Father, on Thee

(December 1967) Mom gave me 'The Talk' a couple of months ago and it was only a matter of time before I was at the age when I was expected to marry. The girls in our community knew what our 'station' was. We were only children for a short time. Then it was our obligation to get married and provide a home for a man who would marry us and give us his name.

We were expected to cook, clean, give him children (preferably sons), and work at any job that would help provide for the family. Some of my friends were maids at a local motel; some went to the mills and factories.

We all learned early that college was a ridiculous thought for 'the likes of us.' We were going to be far too busy for schooling. Most of the young girls dropped out of school by the tenth grade, preparing for marriage. Now it was my turn.

My brother-in-law worked with the man I was told to marry. He was a bully and loud but Mom assured me it was the right thing to do because his people were all hard-working farmers and church-goers.

After the ceremony, my mother walked out of the church and out of my life. We spoke by phone occasionally and I tried to visit her, but there was an incredible wall that came between us. She seemed to believe I had been grafted into a better life and now her responsibility as my mother was over. Even if I never heard her say it, I knew in her heart she loved me and would have given her own life for any of her children. She just never was comfortable with saying the words 'I love you.'

I tried to tell her about my husband's behavior, but she said, "You made your bed; you sleep in it." At first, I was hurt by her words. My heart was breaking as I listened to her casting me off as an abandoned child. ("He healeth the broken in heart, and bindeth up their wounds." Psalm 147:3 KJV).

It was as if she had turned her back on me, not caring what happened to me, but then I realized this was all she had ever known. You prepare for the life you are expected to live and then you just do it …tough it out and don't complain about it… and I really tried to be brave!

He was now my new husband and I had to go and do whatever he decided was best for us, but his intentions for me were anything but honorable. He was physically abusive and I fought my instincts to strike back. I knew he would only get more violent and my pain would be greater. Many times I just ran and hid from him until his anger subsided. I hated being married, but understood it was just what life dealt to me.

I was following the tradition of my ancestors; women learned meekness.("Blessed are the meek: for they shall inherit the earth." Matt.5:5 KJV), but I gained strength and hope by learning another scripture, ("The Lord lifteth up the meek: He casteth the wicked down to the ground." Psalm 147:6 KJV). He promised wives that if they just held on, He would set everything right one way or the other in the home and I received that as His promise to me… and He wants us to take each of His promises as if He were speaking to us personally. That's the personal foundation of all Biblical truth… from One… to one.

(November 1973) My husband was continually out of work. His temper was fiery and he quit his job or was fired monthly. ("Let all bitterness, and wrath, and anger, and clamor, and evil speaking, be put away from you, with all malice: And be ye kind one to another, tenderhearted, forgiving one another, even as God for Christ's sake hath forgiven you." Ephesians 4:31-32 KJV). When you're employed, it's not the boss you need to try to impress; please God, and He will promote you and bless your surroundings.

His mother believed God had given her a son who would be a big, powerful preacher some day, so she overlooked all of his faults. She believed everything he did was acceptable because he was 'called to be a man of God.'

When he abused me, she told me, "Blessed are the peace makers…just try not to annoy him and everything will work out." He was her 'child of promise' so there was always a reason or at least someone else to blame for his actions. She taught him he was entitled to a special set of privileges and everyone in his life had to just stay out of his way. ("Foolishness is bound in the heart of a child, but the rod of correction shall drive it far from him." Prov. 22:15 KJV- "The rod and reproof give wisdom: but a child left to himself bringeth his mother to shame." Prov. 29:15 KJV).

Children are sent to us so we can build strong men and women of God, building blocks for the future, faithful servants of the Lord, but if we teach them to be demanding and temperamental, we only weaken their foundation. Inevitably, they fall …and fail.

Now she believed she could see God at work preparing to take him on his first leg of his evangelical calling, and she was ready for this golden opportunity. His aunt and uncle had a home in Florida and they had become members in a small Pentecostal church located close to their hometown. This was the ideal place for her son, the future preacher, so we moved to Fountain, Florida.

The Springfield Community Church was located about 45 miles from Fountain and the pastor was Rev. J.W. Hunt, a man who walked with God. I was blessed by his wisdom. I had never experienced worship like that. Every service was like a celebration. The music was hand-clapping, toe-tapping spiritual songs that lifted your heart! The testimonial services were full of praise for healings and miracles! ("Praise ye the Lord. Praise God in His sanctuary: praise Him in the firmament of His power. Praise Him for His mighty acts: praise Him according to His excellent greatness. Praise Him with the sound of the trumpet: praise Him with the psaltery and harp. Praise Him with the timbrel and dance: praise Him with stringed instruments and organs. Praise Him upon the loud cymbals: praise Him upon the high sounding cymbals. Let everything that hath breath praise the Lord. Praise ye the Lord." Psalm 150:1-6 KJV).

Within weeks, the bully side of my husband burst forth and I knew our welcome would soon be over. The 'son of promise' would once again be sitting in his mother's farmhouse kitchen in Pennsylvania, looking for a job and a place for his family to live.

She took us in again and again. It was a blessing of sorts, but I knew as long as she was there, he would never be the man he needed to be. ("Wait on the Lord: be of good courage, and He shall strengthen thine heart: WAIT, I say, on the Lord." Psalm 27:14). Only

God could give hope to our sense of futility. I was not accustomed to letting others pay my way through life. I was taught early in life you get just what you work for; anything that comes free or easy is a doorway to trouble!

No one else is responsible for your family but you. That's what makes 'your' family special to you. It belongs to you. If you want what's best for 'your' family, you can avoid a lot of heartache and pitfalls by daily placing them in the hand of God. Ask for His divine guidance as you provide a Christian home for them.

CHAPTER IV

God Created Man on the Sixth Day;
Pain and Suffering Was Not on His Agenda

(August 1978) One morning, I noticed the pain in my knees was becoming excruciating and after tests were performed, the doctor's diagnosis was rheumatoid arthritis, a crippling disease that would leave my body severely handicapped, but God, that Great Physician, decided the diagnosis wasn't final.

After totally relying on a cane for months, He was waiting for me one night at an altar at the Living Waters Church of God in Washington, Pennsylvania. I was so sure my healing would come, I had carved the words, 'Meet My Friend, Jesus,' down the front of my cane. When anyone asked me what it meant, I answered, "Jesus is all I really need to walk, and this cane is only temporary until Jesus takes it away."

One night, the pastor was preaching under a heavy anointing and a teenaged girl had gone up to the altar. I had prayed for months that the young girl would accept Jesus as her Lord and Savior, and now she was kneeling at the altar.

I waited for the group of Christian brothers and sisters to join her at the altar. There were never less than two or three members ready to pray with anyone who came for prayer, but no one moved and she stood there at the altar all alone. I prayed, 'Lord, send someone, anyone to her, to let her know she is loved and we all care about her salvation! Don't let her leave until she's heard from YOU,' but still no one got up from the pew. So I found my cane and made my way to the front of the church.

The preacher saw me approaching and motioned for me to come to him. I pointed to the young girl who had been praying at the altar...but I saw she was standing at the altar, watching me and her face was beaming.

The young minister looked at me and said, "Sister Helen, do

you believe God is going to heal you?" I looked into his eyes and said, "I have no doubt." Again the pastor turned to me and laying his hand upon my head, said, "Lift your hands, Sister, and receive your healing!"

I raised my left hand and started praying but then he stopped me. "Raise BOTH hands, Sister." I started to object because I had relied on that cane to balance me for months. Then I realized, 'If I don't trust God NOW to do His healing, then I would be stealing His Glory and many would be in doubt as to the power of faith in His hands!' So I said quietly, "Father, I give it all to You!"

I raised both my hands, depending on God, and the cane soared back through the air like a projectile! With a resounding "CRACK!" the cane hit the back wall of the sanctuary! My body was entirely healed of rheumatoid arthritis that night. ("He was wounded for our transgressions, He was bruised for our iniquities: The chastisement of our peace was upon Him; and with His stripes we are healed." Isaiah 53:5 KJV).

The congregation had just witnessed a miracle, one of many that was to become a part of my walk with Jesus Christ. The pastor asked if he could keep the cane as a good reminder of that night, and I assured him I had no more use for it. After all, God had done more than healed me. He had taught me a lesson of true priorities.

I do not believe I would have received my healing that night if I had stayed focused on MY needs. My healing was not received until my heart was totally full of compassion for the needs of the young woman who knelt at the altar. ("But whoso hath this world's good, and seeth his brother have need, and shutteth up his bowels of compassion from him, how dwelleth the love of God in him? My little children, let us not love in word, neither in tongue; but in deed and in truth." I John 3:17-18 KJV).

This is a moment of truth for all. If you feel God has turned His back on you in your time of need, I assure you He has not. Sometimes (understanding we are the body of Christ and not just a congregation of interested parties) He requires our voices be used to pray for others, our hands to comfort, our feet to go where He would walk, our eyes to see, and our ears to hear what HE would listen for, if HE were still on earth, walking in the mortal flesh. ("…Behold, to obey is better than sacrifice…" I Samuel 15:22 KJV).

CHAPTER V

'Lost' in a Valley : Or Gaining Strength to Climb Mountains

(May 1980) The Lord had been so good to me. I knew there was a work for me in God's service, but I wasn't sure in what capacity. A minister who was starting a new work in Oklahoma asked if we would come and help him get it established. I jumped at the chance. Soon I was traveling on a Greyhound bus, with three children, headed to Lawton, Oklahoma to become a worker for Christ.

This would be a good time to tell you that not everyone who has a bumper sticker or even a license to preach is necessarily a true Christian. There are many wolves out there ready to consume their own sheep. ("Beware of false prophets, which come to you in sheep's clothing, but inwardly they are ravening wolves." Matt. 7:15 KJV)

Arriving in Oklahoma on a rainy Saturday night, I had expected to be met by my husband and the minister. We, instead, were met by disappointments. The man had been appointed to the church complete with a beautiful parsonage for his family. Until I arrived with the children, my husband stayed with the minister and his family. Every penny we had saved was sent ahead to the church pastor in Oklahoma. The money I had sent on ahead to provide for our housing, was squandered before we arrived. ("Not every one that saith unto me, Lord, Lord, shall enter into the kingdom of heaven; but he that doeth the will of my Father which is in heaven." Matthew 7:21 KJV).

At 11:30 p.m., the minister could not be reached by phone and after calling a cab that reeked of foul odors, the children and I were taken to a motel we could afford on the few dollars I had brought with me to cover any traveling expenses. Needless to say, it was only by the Grace of God we even survived the night.

I rented an apartment for us that had no air conditioning and not even a window fan. In Pennsylvania, I had no air conditioning but this was Oklahoma, and in June the temperature had soared to 110 degrees.

Soon the heat was not the major problem. Our pantry was bare! Three children were hungry and all we had was one egg and two slices of bread. I remember dropping that one egg in a little water, cooking it until I was able to make a spread for the bread. Then I cut the bread into triangles and fed my children the last of our provisions.

My five year old son came to me with tears in his eyes. His little fingers gently tapped my cheek as he said, whispering, "I'm still so hungry, Mama!" I pulled him close to me and told him to go to bed. I promised him that in the morning there would be plenty of food for our breakfast.

I closed the bedroom door, then I dropped to my knees and said, "Lord, my children are hungry and I have nowhere to turn. I'm expecting a miracle from You. My children need food to eat. My heart is breaking seeing them cry for food and I need Your help." ("Though he fall, he shall not be utterly cast down; for the Lord upholdeth him with His hand. I have been young, and now am old; yet have I not seen the righteous forsaken, nor his seed begging bread. He is ever merciful, and lendeth; and his seed is blessed." Psalm 37:24-26 KJV). Before I got to my feet, there was a knock at the door. The 'minister' was struggling as he tried to balance two full bags of groceries. He said, "Someone asked me to bring these groceries to you. I don't know why, but here they are. Good night, now." That 'someone' I will always believe was an angel, sent by God.

That night, my children came out of their bedrooms quicker than Christmas morning and after grace was said, we feasted on manna from heaven! (It may have only been a couple of bologna sandwiches, but to us it was manna!) (He hath given meat unto them that fear Him: He will ever be mindful of His covenant." Psalm 111:5 KJV).

Two months later, we were on our way back to Pennsylvania. When Thanksgiving came that year, we were again sitting back at the farm, being consoled by his mother. She could not believe how unfair that preacher had been to her son.

I had sent fifteen hundred dollars in a certified check to my husband while he was staying at the parsonage, to arrange for our expenses. The check was cashed through the church account, and after they had squandered it, the minister told him he needed to look for a job. Somehow, my mother-in-law felt her son was betrayed. (After all, he was 'supposed to be preaching the gospel' so perhaps the minister should have taken on a layman's job, rather than limit her son's calling).

My minimum wage job at a day care center barely paid the rent on our shabby apartment. There was never a word mentioned again about the cashier's check the man had cashed, nor that he intended to reimburse any of it. My last paycheck paid for the return trip to the farmhouse.

For fifteen years, we seemed destined to spend our lives attached to his parents' farm, although he never felt obliged to put in a day's work there. The children loved their grandparents, but I felt guilty being boarded by the elderly couple. I also didn't approve of the way my husband was pampered. No one was coddled in my family!

Somehow, we needed to start a life of our own where I could freely teach my children the gospel, undiluted by the opinions and attitudes of their grandparents. ("Trust in the Lord with all thine heart; and lean not unto thine own understanding. In all thy ways acknowledge Him, and He shall direct thy paths." Proverbs 3:5-6 KJV).

CHAPTER VI

*Don't Worry About Tomorrow: God's Already There,
Preparing Your Way*

(June 1983) The children were quarreling in the back seat of our rickety Ford station wagon but my thoughts were traveling ahead to our destination. We had sold everything we owned and were going by faith to Florida.

My father died in 1972, and this year Mom died at the age of 61. It seemed as if there was nothing left in Pennsylvania for us but grief and poverty. Factories were closing due to the economy. Steel mills were once the life's breath of the area but now they were just cemeteries of dead dreams behind cold security gates. Coal mines, where generations of men and women had dedicated, and in many sad cases, given their lives, were now shut down like unmarked graves.

Families remembered the Great Depression and feared the worst for their families. It was a state of dark despair and I knew the only way to avoid giving up, as so many of my neighbors had, was to take a risk and strike out to new opportunities.

I prayed God would open doors and lead us to His perfect plan for our lives. I found a map and seeing, 'Gainesville, Florida,' wondered if we had anything to 'gain' by circling that city on the map as our destination. I decided we had nothing to lose. Somehow, I just knew Gainesville would be a momentous place for us. The last winter we closed off most of the house, heating just two rooms, but we still huddled in blankets day and night to keep warm. Florida was sounding better all the time.

I knew this would mean leaving my brothers and my older sister behind in Pennsylvania. ("Now the Lord had said unto Abram, Get thee out of thy country, and from thy kindred, and from thy father's house, unto a land that I will shew thee: And I will make of thee a great nation, and I will bless thee, and make thy name great; and thou shalt be a blessing:" Gen.12:1-2 KJV).

(October 1985) I stood in our yard in Newberry, Florida, and listened as the police woman gave me all the details of the day's events, but all I could hear was a buzz that seemed to drown out her voice. My mind had gone into survival mode and I found myself babbling about laundry and cooking and anything that could distract me from facing the facts she had presented to me. My husband had been arrested for raping our daughter…INCEST! How did it happen …when… why…where…HOW did this happen?

I knew he was a loud bully and his aggression was just something I had learned to live with…I thought. I received many blows that were aimed at our children and at times I just grabbed them and ran as far and as fast as I could, into other rooms or out of his reach until he calmed down. ("The God of my rock; in Him will I trust: He is my shield and the horn of my salvation, my high tower, and my refuge, my savior; Thou savest me from violence." II Samuel 22:3 KJV).

I'm not going to say I stayed with him because he had so many redeeming qualities. I never saw any. From birth, this had been my destiny and no amount of my protesting changed the custom: I married him for life and this was 'the bed in which I had to sleep.' Only my prayer time brought me peace. ("…In Me ye might have peace…" John 16:33 KJV).

Now this one day brought the biggest change in our lives. The bully, the man who owned me, who bellowed he was the master of our house…was gone for good. He was arrested and taken immediately to jail. The state assisted me in filing for divorce. He was never going to hurt any of us again. Now it was just the children and me… AND GOD!

I looked through tear swollen eyes and somehow saw the most beautiful blue sky I had ever seen. I took a deep breath and felt freedom! I realized this must be how it felt to have been a captive in battle and rescued. For seventeen long years, I had fought an enemy in my own home … beaten, raped and sodomized! I was tortured at times into submission and crouched in fear each time he raised his voice. Now that was all in the past. My children would be safe and loved.

The future was very frightening. Would I be able to raise a family alone? I had no education and all my work experience was as menial labor. I had waited tables, worked in factories, and on a dairy farm with the family, but none of my work experience would be enough to provide for my family!

For years, my husband insisted I could never leave him because I couldn't make it without him and no other man would ever want me. He constantly berated me and humiliated me, trying to destroy any self-worth I might have retained. How foolish he was to have wasted the effort; my upbringing already taught me I had no value except to make a man's life comfortable. ("Who can find a virtuous woman? For her price is far above rubies. The heart of her husband doth safely trust in her, so that he shall have no need of spoil." Prov. 31:10-11 KJV). Yet to my husband, I was a burden.

I remember the four of us sitting huddled together in the waiting room of the hospital, like four wild rabbits cornered by a dangerous presence. I promised my three children only good things would come. We vowed to each other that day or night, we would be there for each other. If anyone needed to talk or cry or just scream…any of us would be available.

My oldest son, Jimmy, was seventeen and worked at a Burger King restaurant after school and on weekends. He said, "Mom, I know it isn't much, but you can count on my money for the budget." My daughter was going to help more with the housework and my youngest said he wanted to try to find odd jobs in the neighborhood. With my job at Pic N Save, together, we would make it. There might not be any luxuries, but I felt like the richest woman in the world at that moment. I was truly blessed.

The following Monday, HRS entered my home while I was at work and took my two younger children with any possessions they believed might belong to the children they were abducting. They were placed in a shelter where they could be 'protected.' I was hysterical and fury had a new meaning that day! I was madder than a mother bear whose cubs were taken. I tried to turn to scripture and all I kept reading was "Cease from anger, and forsake wrath; do not fret - it leads only to evil." Psalm 37:8 KJV. I cried, "Lord, my children have been stolen and I don't know where they are!"

I received an anonymous call that night from an officer of the court who told me he could be fired if anyone found out he had contacted me. He said there would be a court hearing the next day and it would be in my best interest to be there.

The county courthouse was four miles away and I had to get an early start. No one knew when our case would be called on the docket and I had to walk to get to court. (I had no car at the time.) I had to take time off from work even though every penny had already been budgeted.

I was in for the battle of my life. I wanted someone to tell me what to do, what to say, where to turn! I prayed and waited to hear the state authorities explain what was going on. ("The eyes of the Lord are in every place, beholding the evil and the good." Prov. 15:3 KJV). I could hardly believe my ears as I heard them read the 'facts' of the case, each numerically listed:

1. I lost custody of my children because the authorities believed we were under too much stress. We all 'relied too heavily on each other' to recover from our crisis, implying that our unity was a bad sign. (My view was we were stronger and healing together as a family).

2. They believed I was financially incapable of raising three children. I believed with God all things are possible. Besides, we were all committed to making it work. Ecclesiastes 4:12, says, 'a threefold cord is not easily broken.' (I mentally pictured God, with my children and me ~ a threefold cord, an unbeatable set.)

3. They believed I worked too many hours to be with my children in their time of stress. (I believed my work ethics were an example to my children who vowed to help each other through our problems). ("The desire of the slothful [lazy] killeth him; for his hands refuse to labour." Proverbs 21:25 KJV). Proverbs speaks well of a woman who takes care of her family: ("She looketh well to the ways of her household, and eateth not the bread of idleness." Proverbs 31:27 KJV).

4. The court appointed counselor believed I needed to seek out a male companion so the children would not be fearful of the traditional two-parent home. I said I was too busy and not ready to socialize, to which their reply was perhaps I needed less pressure to provide for my children and to experience dating. I rejected all her recommendations. They were hard to take, considering the therapist was a divorced woman in her fifties who had lost custody of her

own children to her ex-husband. ("And He spake a parable unto them, 'Can the blind lead the blind? Shall they not both fall into the ditch'?" Luke 6:39 KJV).

Two days later, I stopped for a cup of coffee with a fellow employee who tried to console me. The next day, there was a court date where the counselor claimed I was socializing, therefore expressing no genuine concern for my children. I was on a treacherous seesaw, not knowing which way to shift my weight. I spent my days working for every penny I could get and every night in earnest prayer, tears filling my pillow as I mourned the loss of my children. I had spent my entire life defensively and as their mother, I shielded them daily from the dangers and evils we endured. Now I was in a battle with the people who 'rescued' us. In this war, I wasn't sure of the rules or who my allies were. I had no idea what my next move would be.

All I knew for sure was God was still watching over us. ("Lord, how are they increased that trouble me! Many are they that rise up against me." Ps.3:1 KJV "But Thou, O Lord, art a shield for me; my glory, and the lifter up of mine head." Ps.3:3 KJV "I laid me down and slept; I awakened; for the Lord sustained me." Ps.3:5 KJV).

Doris, a new advocate for children in the court's Guardian Ad Litem Program, decided to befriend me and my children. She said it would be her ultimate goal to bring my family back together where we belonged, and even though she appeared to enjoy my children, warning flags were waving all over my mothering defense.

I had a real trust issue at this point in my life. ("Trust in the Lord with all thine heart; and lean not unto thine own understanding. In all thy ways acknowledge Him, and He shall direct thy paths." Prov. 3:5-6 KJV). I knew if God did not remove my doubts, I was not about to let down my guard. He would always be my strength.

I had loved and protected my children all my life. Guilt had dealt a hard blow to me when my daughter was raped and I, being so foolishly naïve, had overlooked the signs. Now, nothing was about to get past me again!

I treasured my oldest son, who had stood by me since he was a little boy. I have had awful nightmares where I relived the night in 1978 when he sat rigid, vowing to kill his father for the way he hurt us and called us names. No ten year old should have to experience such pain. I swallowed hard and forced a slight laugh as I said, "We don't care what he calls us! If he called you a purple cow, would you moo and give grape juice?" Then he giggled as I tickled him.

I told him his dad had to live with himself and his own meanness, but we were going to rise above it and not be like him. Solemnly he agreed, but I relived his threat for years as I anguished for a solution.

Now we walked through each room in our home without dodging a kick or some object being thrown and we no longer had to hide and whisper so he couldn't hear us talking, but it was the state of Florida who took away our attacker. I was just not strong enough to do it on my own. I didn't even realize I had any options! Even though I had to walk down several dark valleys, I remembered the twenty-third Psalm, when nothing else came to mind to give me peace through troubled times. ("The Lord is my Shepherd; I shall not want. He maketh me to lie down in green pastures: He leadeth me beside the still waters. He restoreth my soul: He leadeth me in the paths of righteousness for His name's sake. Yea, though I walk through the valley of the shadow of death, I will fear no evil: for Thou art with me; Thy rod and Thy staff they comfort me. Thou preparest a table before me in the presence of mine enemies: Thou anointest my head with oil; my cup runneth over. Surely goodness and mercy shall follow me all the days of my life: and I will dwell in the house of the Lord for ever." Ps. 23 KJV).

I wondered if there would ever be a time when we wouldn't feel threatened by someone or something. ("But they that wait upon the Lord shall renew their strength; they shall mount up with wings as eagles; they shall run, and not be weary; and they shall walk, and not faint." Isaiah 40:31 KJV).

Now my eldest son was a young man, handsome, strong, and intelligent. He was so skilled with computers, the teachers at his high school sought his help. My daughter was still the rebellious one, testing anyone in authority; but my youngest son amazed everyone.

When he was tested for emotional stability (or lack of it), he decided to make it into a game. As the child psychologist tried to analyze him, he laughed. He colored the flowers black, drew a giant spaceship with various colors of raindrops bombarding him and even put in lightning bolts for good measure. Then he explained he knew they were going to seek out violent tendencies in his artistic endeavors, so he wanted to give them something to think about.

He was in a group home, called Interface at the time, for children from troubled homes. He was there for less than a day when he figured out the reward system was a 'no-brainer' for him. While the social workers were attempting to instill positive behavior in their residents, my son, Daniel, co-operated without any problems.

At home, he had learned to go directly to the kitchen when he got off the bus, finish his homework (requiring a complete review of all his finished work), followed by putting away his school supplies, washing up and getting the table ready for the evening meal. He always assisted in clearing the table and clean up. Then he could watch a show on television or have a couple hours of free time.

Each morning, when he got up, he made his bed before getting ready for school, and his clothes were always laid out the night before. Now, at Interface, the counselors were insisting he learn good behavioral skills to improve his life. Yet there was not one behavior problem they could modify, except he insisted he should be allowed to go back home.

They rewarded him by paying certain amounts of allowances for each good habit he demonstrated by his chores and life style. Soon they became annoyed, seeing they were paying him money for something they hadn't taught him.

He just wanted to go home with his mother, and no matter what horrible things we had to face, he knew he was going to stand by my side. He just had a child's faith that even if the family was going through a crisis, we loved the Lord and that meant we were relying on an infallible God with a plan to carry us through this dark period of our lives. He promised through His covenant to provide for us in our troubled times that He may receive our praises for His mercy. ("But ye are a chosen generation, a royal priesthood, an holy nation, a peculiar people; that ye should shew forth the praises of Him who hath called you out of darkness into His marvelous light." 1 Peter 2:9 KJV).

I knew soon, this trial would be behind us because someone once said to me, "God never gives us more than we can bear." I was beginning to falter and as I reached out to God, He said to my heart, "This IS more than YOU can bear. But I will never give you more than you and I, TOGETHER, can bear. Lean on me." And a peace swept over me, refreshing my spirit. ("Come unto me, all ye that labor and are heavy laden, and I will give you rest. Take my yoke upon you, and learn of me; for I am meek and lowly in heart: and ye shall find rest unto your souls. For my yoke is easy, and my burden is light." Matthew 11-28-30 KJV).

CHAPTER VII

You Can't Get Lost: God Will Guide You Home

(December 22nd 1987) The next day would be my wedding day. Doris was the newest member of the Guardian Ad Litem group. She told me she had found a way to get my children back for me, but it would mean that I had to get married again.

A man named Robert had brought me home from Lillie's Place, where I had been selling cakes, cookies and candy. I found if I got home from work at six at night, I could bake and make fudge until eight. The next night I sold my baked goods to local cafes and sandwich shops. It wasn't much, but every penny counted on my tight budget.

The ride home meant I could be with my son (and soon the other two children) for an hour or so before going to bed. When Doris heard about 'unmarried Robert,' her eyes started to dance! "That's it." she said, "that's how we get your kids back home!" I was too tired to make much sense of what she was saying, but I knew I heard the word 'marry' because my stomach knotted up and I felt nauseated.

She told me the only thing that would make the authorities believe my home was suitable would be if I was moving on with my life, and a new husband would clinch the deal. I prayed for a miracle that would bring me a new alternative, but none came.

Doris told Robert her plan and he was willing to marry me to get my children back home with me, but I wasn't through with the negotiations yet. He assured me I had nothing about which to worry; he just wanted to help me. He was divorced, too, and he had been sleeping on the garage floor in his brother's house. All he owned was in one brown paper bag, and even the blanket he used at his brother's house belonged to his brother. He didn't even own a pillow, but he did have an old Ford truck.

Doris and Robert were quick to remind me I wouldn't have to

walk all the way to the bus stop anymore, and I had to admit in the summer storms and the winter cold, a ride was an answered prayer, but the most important thing was that my family would be reunited.

Doris said, "I made a background check on Robert to assure he was trustworthy, not a serial killer, and..." she added, with a chuckle, "not already married." She laughed to make light of any new objections I might have come up with. Then the plans were put into action for the most unusual wedding of all time, but I was granted 'temporary custody' of my children.

The preacher came to the house where my three children were getting acquainted with their new five year old step-sister, Robert's daughter. He said he wanted his daughter to have all the benefits of a real family and her mother agreed to give him full custody.

I had chosen a dress from the consignment shop where I worked and Robert had a new shirt and dress slacks. We even had a wedding cake on the kitchen table, (I baked it the night before), but when the minister started to read the marriage vows, I excused myself, sat down at the kitchen table and stared at my ugly cake through tear-filled eyes.

Robert called to me, but I told him to go on without me. I knew I had married him because I called out "YES!" from the kitchen when I heard the preacher say 'do you?' Then the 'wedding' was over, the preacher was gone, and there was no turning back. I sadly looked at the man who became my husband and my children's new step-father. He was a... virtual stranger. How could this mess happen?

I changed my clothes and went back to work at the PVC pipe plant where I had been working for the last couple of months. I had just become a married woman again and I could almost hear my mother's foreboding voice saying, "You made your bed, now sleep in it!"

December faded away in sorrow and almost nine years later I sat in another HRS office. A young teenaged girl had been raped by her father and I was there to tell them what I knew about it. And again, I was dumfounded. Were these perverted abusers really that clever or was I that stupid? Naïve? Gullible? Did I magnetically attract them?

Robert was nothing like my first husband. In my first marriage, our daughter seemed to be a possession that belonged only to him. He tried to hurt her several times the same way he struck out in anger at our sons, but I was able to rescue her from his anger most of the time. I never saw any sexual contact, but she was the only child he ever tolerated at all. He bought her gifts and he even took her side when she didn't want to do her chores, often reassigning them to one or both of the boys.

However, Robert distanced himself from his daughter. He never wanted to include her in any conversation and he rejected any affection she showed him. He said he knew what I went through with my first husband and he never wanted me to have any distrust with him. He always believed my daughter probably lied about her father and sent him to prison. Robert believed if he kept his distance, he would never be accused. I made sure he knew the evidence was what sent Patty's father to prison, not her accusation, which was proven as fact, but I really didn't care what he believed about anything!

Yet as I stared at the clock on the wall, I recognized the same paper calendar attached… the same month and day and even the same hour, like some crazy déjà vu! Ten years ago I was in the same horrific situation. The mother was contacted and took custody of her daughter. I told her I was not the one she needed now. I had to get my life realigned with some kind of reality and she needed her birth mother.

The authorities started to question me and just like the first time, I was presented with the hard facts, which were, "We demand your co-operation or we will exercise our right to remove all of your children into foster care." I remembered those days and the sacrifices and all the nightmares I had suffered; even my marriage to a man I didn't love, later didn't like, and now I didn't respect at all. I was trapped by a system I didn't understand. ("For yet a little while, and the wicked shall not be: yea, thou shalt diligently consider his place, and it shall not be." Psalm 37:10 KJV).

Now there was one thing I knew for sure. I was a much more confident woman this time. I felt my blood boil! I heard myself say, "My 'children' are twenty-seven, twenty-five, and twenty-two. None of them live at home and you can't have my children this time. My youngest son is in the United States Army and they won't release him to you or anyone else. Now I am going home."

The caseworker closed his mouth, which was gaping open and replied, "You need to wait for your husband. I think they are just about done with his questioning. He admitted his guilt so it's all procedure now."

I remember putting my hands on my hips and repeating, " 'I' am going home. Whatever you decide to do with him is between you and him. I have no husband and he has no home with me. Now I am leaving… !" and I walked away.

I drove two miles to a Jeep dealer where we had purchased a Jeep Cherokee, (the vehicle of his choice six months prior to this terrible day). It never mattered to him I didn't want the vehicle. It was too expensive and impractical for my needs. I traded it in for a new Plymouth Neon I could afford and drove to my home…alone.

CHAPTER VIII

The Spirit Whispers, 'Touch Me', and You'll Never Be Alone Again

(October 1995) I was indeed alone…again. The sun had just set and now the darkened skies seemed to drape over my home like a shroud. There were no sounds of laughter or voices that exchanged trivial anecdotes of the day's events. It had been years since I heard, "Hey. Mom, can I…?" Just silence.

My sons were grown and had dedicated their lives to God; their homes were centered around Jesus Christ. My daughter was still wandering, trying to find answers to just where she fit into this unsettling world where she was constantly at war. She had not yet found her peace and she trusted no one but those like her.

She was like a child of the night. The darkness was her haven where she hid, afraid of the light where her abusive father was the enemy yet controller of her life…the light where her own mother claimed peace through Jesus Christ. Yet this higher power seemed to do nothing to save her daughter from her tortured spirit.

Other rebellious teens and young adults became her trusted 'family' and the laws did not pertain to them and their survival. Drugs had clouded their troubled minds and shoplifting was a way to pay for their immediate needs.

Days were spent behind closed doors, recovering from snorting cocaine, smoking pot or drunken orgies. Communes developed as these misfits gathered together (children raising their own children) with no thoughts of the future; only dependency on each other and their chemical addictions.

Each new day offered only deeper withdrawals into a world of darkness. Still, I prayed. ("For we wrestle not against flesh and blood, but against principalities, against powers, against the rulers of the darkness of this world, against spiritual wickedness in high places." Ephesians 6:12 KJV).

My daughter was not in this battle alone. Daily, I grabbed my

'Sword,' (the Word of God), and battled for her soul. The night seemed to last forever, as I prayed for my little girl's soul to seek salvation. Then those nights extended into weeks. My friends told me to leave it alone. I needed to stop worrying. She was going to do whatever she wanted and if she hurt me, well, then, it was just an added bonus to her. Some tried to comfort me by saying I had done the best I could and now it was up to her to make the right decision. If she died and went to hell, well, I had done my best and it wouldn't be my fault. Whose fault wasn't the issue. I wanted a miracle for my child!

No one seemed able to look past my pain to see the promise God made to me. I did! He promised my children would be saved! Not two out of three…all of them! My so-called well-wishers wanted me to just give up? I recalled Job's reply to his visitors. ("Behold now, I have ordered my cause; I know that I shall be justified." Job 13:18 KJV). I knew for what I was praying and I expected God would honor my request! ("For all the promises of God in Him are yea, and in Him Amen, unto the glory of God by us." 2 Corinthians 1:20 KJV).

Even in the days of Job there were doubters who wanted him to accept his agony as retribution. Some believed it was God's will he should suffer without expecting God to move on his behalf. and Job replied, "Withdraw thine hand far from me: and let not thy dread make me afraid." (Job 13:21 KJV). Fear is the opposite of faith and I knew if I allowed those around me to speak defeat, then half the battle was already lost!

When Paul and Silas were in prison in Philippi, God sent a great earthquake that loosed the foundations of the prison, and Paul and Silas were set free from their shackles, but the guard was so scared he was ready to take his own life when Paul shouted out to him telling him his prisoners had not fled. So the guard fell down before Paul and Silas. ("And brought them out and said, 'Sirs, what must I do to be saved?' And they said, 'Believe on the Lord Jesus Christ, and thou shalt be saved, AND THY HOUSE.' " Acts 16:30-31 KJV).

I knew by God's Word that when I believed in the Lord Jesus Christ, I 'AND MY HOUSE' would be saved, and I was still standing on that promise! Every time I heard the telephone ring, my throat tightened as I waited to hear that maybe my daughter had been found overdosed or killed. Is this lack of faith? I know it to be the fear all mothers have when their children are out in sin…and I prayed even more.

I knew what she was facing and how dangerous her life had become. She refused to listen to my pleas to trust Jesus, but unlike Job's visitors, I knew God had a plan, just like at Philippi's earthquake, to answer a heartfelt prayer.

At the time, I could do nothing to resolve my daughter's plight and even my own life felt empty now. No one seemed to need me anymore and I was drowning in self pity. I knew it was very important to find something productive to do with my life or else trouble would be waiting for me. I remembered in high school I was required to read Chaucer, a 12th century writer who said, 'Idle hands are the devil's tools.' I knew I had a strong personal relationship with the Lord but I also knew that if Jesus Christ was attacked by Satan's temptations, then I surely was not home-free yet.

I prayed hard each time someone invited me out, knowing I would be entertained by someone who had a different lifestyle than mine. Rather than explaining my beliefs and value system, I declined all invitations. Now they just stopped asking me.

(November 1995) Thanksgiving was being celebrated in the park for the homeless so I dressed warmly and volunteered to serve the needy. I felt wonderful after they had been fed but as the volunteers sat down to eat, I excused myself and went home.

I had suddenly realized everyone was talking about the evening meals they would be having with their husbands and family. I was as alone as the homeless men and women we had fed. It just didn't feel right to me. How did I manage to be so alone?

My purpose in life was gone. I missed taking care of family, making home cooked meals, sewing and baking favorite cookies and tucking someone in at night. I stood in the cool night air that evening and I do believe I heard a train whistle in the distance. Pulling the collar of my coat up around my ears, I tried to bring back memories of the scent of the coarse blankets we had as children. I remembered on wash day Mom dragged out the old wringer washer and the Twenty Mule Team Borax.

I closed my eyes, begging those old time train whistles to be recalled back from my memory. I needed to dream of happy destinations and angels listening to those gospel singers at heaven's gates. ("O God, Thou hast taught me from my youth: and hitherto have I declared Thy wondrous works." Psalm 71:17 KJV). 'Mama, sing just one more song, and I know I'll be okay,' but Mama was gone. 'Father, comfort me.'

CHAPTER IX

*Surrender Breaks Down Walls Between
Hardened Hearts and God's Love*

As I walked down the narrow corridor of that single-wide trailer, Robert's words echoed in my tortured mind, remembering the deposition he had given the police officers when he was arrested for raping his daughter and incestuous battery on a minor child. Every room held an evil haunting message as he detailed his activities with his daughter throughout our home. I shivered as I stopped in front of the fireplace.

How I loved to stand at the hearth and tell my little four year old granddaughter the nativity story. There came a sense of shame over me as I realized I had never left my granddaughter alone with Robert and yet his own daughter was being victimized by him.

Why had I not seen her abuse? I considered my granddaughter was MY personal responsibility and I never wanted her to be disciplined by Robert. Knowing his lack of patience with little children, I made sure he never had the chance to be abusive with my granddaughter. Yet in shame, I had to acknowledge my failure to protect the other young girl in my care.

I never interfered when he disciplined his daughter, even when I disagreed with his harsh punishment. I just vowed he would never touch one of my own family. I had no idea of the true pain he inflicted on his own daughter. Now, I seemed to be destined to witness the ghostly heinous acts over and over in this single-wide trailer, his den of iniquity and debauchery.

As the sun descended, I grabbed my jacket and left that place and drove away to a better place…any place that quieted the haunting memories of a sobbing little girl whose life was altered forever by the one person who was assigned by God to be her protector, her Daddy.

The night air was crisp and even though Christmas would soon be here, there was not even one 'Joyeaux Noel' in me. For years, I argued the fact that those who used the phrase, Merry X-mas obviously had never met Mr. X, but this year was different. I did not care who greeted whom for the holidays or anything else.

Everywhere I looked I saw fathers I didn't trust; mothers who just quite possibly may have been heading for my bad experiences. I searched for hints in the faces of the children who may have been too scared to confront their abusers. Every crying child tore at my heart as I gazed suspiciously at the parents.

I looked in my rear view mirror and realized I hardly recognized the woman who was staring back at me. Her eyes were cold and untrusting. I saw no fear but I did see anger... lots and lots of anger! I felt like crying but what good would it do? Yes, Mama, I made my bed... but this time I had help.

Now what? I was out at night going nowhere, to see no one, and had nothing to say to anyone if I met someone, anyhow! GOD! HELP ME! Is this how it feels to go insane? There was no one to help now...just...God...("...For He hath said, I will never leave thee, nor forsake thee." Hebrews 13:5b KJV. "For in the time of trouble He shall hide me in His pavilion: in the secret of His tabernacle shall He hide me; He shall set me up upon a rock. And now shall mine head be lifted up above mine enemies round about me: therefore will I offer in His tabernacle sacrifices of joy; I will sing, yea, I will sing praises unto the Lord." Psalms 27: 5-6 KJV).

But now all I heard was the shallow sobbing that came from my chest, so full of pain, aching and tired, having spent all the energy left inside of me. I was deeply burdened but I had nowhere to go to find the rest for my weary body, and I couldn't face going home. That verse echoed in my brain: "...I will sing unto the Lord; I will sing praise to the Lord God of Israel." (Judges 5:3 KJV). Yet this dark night held nothing but silence; not even another living soul appeared to be on the highway this night.

I rolled down my window to let in some fresh air but it didn't help my mood. Then suddenly, I saw a flash of light to my left and I heard a woman's laughter as she flirted playfully with a young man exiting a building on Main Boulevard.

As soon as I approached the turning lane, I entered the parking lot without even giving it a second thought. There was music in that building and the people were enjoying the night! They weren't miserable like me and something inside of me was drawn to them like a moth to a flame.

I closed the driver's door on my car and the sound of it made me stop and think. It was around midnight and the music and laughter coming from inside could only mean trouble to a Christian woman out alone at night.

I was feeling strong enough with all the pent up anger to take on the devil himself, and besides, I was over twenty-one (at least twice over twenty-one). I had no intention of consuming alcohol nor carousing with men. I just craved the noise which might be able to drown out my tortured thoughts that raced through my mind… just for the night.

I satisfied my doubts with the conviction I would sit alone and drink water or Coke if the establishment seemed to be bothered by my presence. Then I gave myself a good shake and marched inside like the spies with Joshua, fearfully predicting defeat but boldly exploring the territory. ("Be strong and of a good courage, fear not, nor be afraid of them: for the Lord thy God, He it is that doth go with thee; He will not fail thee, nor forsake thee." Deut. 31:6 KJV).

"Hello, I saw you sitting here alone and thought you might like some company." A middle aged man had approached me, and he obviously had too many drinks already. I definitely had no need for his company or anyone else's for that matter, but I knew my manners. "I really just came in to listen to the music. I'm not good company tonight. I'm sorry."

I turned the bar stool away from him. "I've never seen you in here before. Are you from around here?" I was beginning to feel annoyed. "I'm from Ellisville, but if you don't mind, I just want to sit here by myself…alone…PLEASE?"

Again, he approached me, "Did you drive here tonight, or did someone bring you? What kind of a car do you have? I have a great car and I have some land in Ohio."

I couldn't believe how much information he was giving me, a total stranger. Now he was opening his wallet but I couldn't tell if he was trying to show me all his pictures or show off all his credit cards in his possession, since they all cascaded into his lap. I had no more patience with this intruder so I said, "Look, I told you I didn't want company, but you won't listen. I don't want to be rude, but I really do not care what you own, or drive or what cards you have. I don't need anything from you so please just go away!" The hostility I showed was unusual for me and my voice shrilled.

The lady bartender laughed and said, "I guess she told you! You better go now while she's willing to let you walk away without a fight! I think she can take you." I rubbed my forehead to try to ease the pressure before I got up from the counter to leave.

Then, I heard a humble voice that said, "I'm sorry. It's my fault he bothered you. He kept hanging around over there with me and I sent him to you to get rid of him."

The intruder was trying to get back onto the bar stool he left while trying to retrieve his credit cards, but the new visitor blocked his passageway. "Look, if we walk away, he might take the hint and leave you alone. Let's go over to the dance floor." I protested but he didn't hear me.

The band was playing on the stage nearby. I started to shake my head to tell him I wasn't much for dancing. Exactly how was I going to explain that I have danced … (in the Spirit) at our anointed revivals and services? Of course, there were no barroom bands and definitely no scantily dressed drink servers!

I tried to look around the room for the exit but the place was packed with party goers and couples hugging each other. I turned around once to see how far I was from the door I entered and noticed the room was beginning to feel less crowded. We were on the dance floor but the others seemed to drift off in other directions.

The lead singer with the band said they were going to slow things down a bit and then he started to sing a new country song called, 'Keeper of the Stars.' I glanced around and saw we were alone on the dance floor. I felt conspicuous but the man who introduced himself as 'Danny' told me to just relax and follow him.

It seemed the words to the song were being spoken directly to us…"He sure knew what He was doing…when He brought these two hearts together," and I realized that here in this unlikely place, God was being praised as the 'Keeper of the stars!'

That was just the first night of many when Danny comforted me and assured me he would take care of me. He had met me that night when I was desperate for God's intervention. I had met him that night when he was wondering if there wasn't a little something better in life than going to the bars every night and guessing when his 'luck' would run out and he would be just another statistic for the coroner.

Danny had his driving privileges revoked when he was in his early twenties for drunk driving. Now he had become accustomed to being a passenger in cars driven by other drunken drivers who had not yet been cited for DUI. It was just a matter of time before he was found dead from alcohol abuse or an accident.

As far as I was concerned, I felt safe with him. I knew with his past run-ins with the law and the bar's night life he enjoyed, I was not about to bring him into my world!

Somehow, despite my reluctance to get involved with him, I knew he needed to be rescued and I needed someone to take care of… 'a friend in need.' It appeared to be a perfect equation for us.

We both knew we were not experiencing love at first sight, but he says now, "God sent an angel into the bar to rescue me." I remember a very different miracle. ("Be not forgetful to entertain strangers: for thereby some have entertained angels unawares." Heb. 13:2 KJV).

Danny was the man God sent into my life when I needed a shoulder to lean on; someone to balance out my life, to be the strength in my weakness. Yet he demanded nothing in return.

He just became my best friend. I saw I could help make his life feel safer and more fulfilling. I needed to have someone who would make me feel needed. I wasn't used to having no one depend on me. He enjoyed the meals I cooked and without a driver's license, he was always grateful I was available to drive him wherever he wanted to go. Many times that meant I took him to the bar-rooms where I sat and drank coke or water. He drank beer and whiskey.

I never tried to make him over or preach to him. ("Brethren, be followers together of me, and mark them which walk so as ye have for an ensample." Philippians 3:17 KJV). I just drove and appreciated having someone to talk to, but soon he was less comfortable in the bars. He began to hear the joke tellers repeat the same jokes over and over again. He was aware of the slurred voices and women who flirted openly. He was also viewing them as dangerous liaisons. He was getting tired of going to the bars, and started to notice something different about me. He became uncomfortable around the women in the bar, embarrassed when they approached him.

One day, after an older friend he knew from his childhood invited him to church, he accepted, although he had declined twice on previous invitations. I was very happy to see God move in his life. (God said to wait upon Him for His timing was perfect!)

I knew he was searching for more meaning in his life but I knew if I dragged him to the church where I found my peace, I could put him back in the bars again. ("The Lord is good unto them that wait for Him, to the soul that seeketh Him." Lament. 3:25 KJV).

So, as he once told me that night a couple of years before, 'Relax and follow me,' I followed him to church. I watched him grow into a strong man of godly values.

CHAPTER X

Awesome Blessings Come to Those Who Wait On God's Direction

(May 1ˢᵗ, 1999) We were married at the Southside Baptist Church in Lake City, Florida, on a Saturday afternoon. The church was building a new sanctuary and we were the last wedding to be celebrated in the old section. For some reason, that brought a sense of pride to us. It was almost as if the purpose for the longevity of that sacred place was to stand and wait for us.

After we were joined by God's blessing, it was allowed to rest as the congregation gathered into the new structure, designed for worshippers who were impressed with the grandeur of the architectural design. They were in awe of the domed ceiling but we had a place in our heart for the little church where we became husband and wife.

We shared our thoughts and ideas and even our beliefs in God's plan for our lives together. Ultimately, we knew without a doubt God had planned a move for us as we started on our spiritual walk with Him. We prayed together and committed our lives to Him daily as we became more humble and submissive, willing to follow Him wherever He led us. We agreed we would walk only in the paths He set before us, and the blessings were abundant.

The months that followed our May wedding were very eventful. In July, we were signing the bank papers to buy our own home. This in itself does not sound miraculous, but every part of the transaction was guided by the hand of God.

One day in March, before we were married, Danny and I were sitting on the porch of an old share-cropper's house, located in the middle of a pasture where a herd of beef cattle grazed. We realized, as we were being counseled by the pastor, we had to stay away from the temptation of living together before marriage, but we were together every day until dusk, when I returned to my son's home where I had previously moved.

We talked a lot about the years we struggled through before we met at Tom's. We made plans for the wedding and the honeymoon. We even made plans for the future we would share (after the celebrations). There were three in our conversation that day. Danny and I were in the presence of God, the Father, who was listening to the heart's desires of His children.

Danny never had much of a childhood, being responsible for six younger brothers and sisters plus the cousins who moved in with them with his Aunt Darlene. He told me how hard it was to have anything of his own unless he locked it up in a footlocker. So all his valued possessions and keepsakes were always packed away out of sight.

He dreamed someday of having an entire room to set out all his things where he could sit and appreciate them for as long as he wanted to admire them, but his selection of treasure had always been minimal, amounting to what could fit in one locked trunk.

Lately, I had been finding collectible miniature cars and trucks, and the sparkle in his eye was reward enough. He was enjoying a time in his life he had never been able to experience as a child, and I was blessed to share these rewarding moments with him.

One dream we shared was a home where he could enjoy his privacy and have everything he valued protected yet on display like a precious museum piece. There would never be any danger that his possessions would be stolen or damaged, not in 'our' home!

The home we verbally designed that day would have to be close to town. Since I was the lifelong designated driver, the cost of travel would double for us driving to the different job sites. Then, after the location was agreed upon, we also chose to have a very private residence, even if it was inside the city limits.

We disliked even the most elite neighborhoods where all the houses were built so close together, they ended up sharing the adjacent lot. Jokingly, we commented we would have to learn to whisper a lot in some of those developments to keep all the neighbors from hearing our conversations.

By now, we were enjoying the game we had started as we planned our dream house. There would be ceiling fans everywhere. I swatted at a mosquito and Danny added, "Well, let's not forget the screened-in porch, to keep out the mosquitoes."

We stood and looked out over the pasture land and saw the hogwire fence, which brought us to agree our home would be all fenced in but not like that. We decided we preferred a chain link fence around our private lot, in town, at the house with many ceiling fans and a porch that was screened in so we could sit outside at night and not be bothered by mosquitoes.

We weren't done yet. There had to be a big yard where he could work on cars if he wanted. In fact, it would be really nice if there were even a garage or building where two cars could be parked or worked on…two bays, what a dream! That area of the lot would most definitely have to be fenced off as well, to keep out any unwanted visitors.

That night when we said our farewells, we smiled as we closed the book of our dreams. Neither of us had any savings of which to speak and at this point, pleasant dreams were all we had to hold onto, but we had a Father who was very generous with the blessings for His children.

(July 1999) God showed His miraculous love for us. We were getting ready to move into our new home. We saw a classified ad that listed a house on a corner lot, and it sounded like our dream home, just a few blocks from the center of town. I read it twice before showing the ad to my husband. He smiled and said, "I think we had better go and check it out today."

There was one chain link fence around the house and a second was around the two empty lots next to it. In fact, a two-bay workshop (equipped with water and electricity) was located on the back of the adjacent lots.

A drive-through gate opened into the parcel of land next to the house and a walk-through gate opened into the front yard of the home and still another small gate was at the front by the mailbox …a real home… with a screened-in porch that held a ceiling fan.

This home had a separate room off the front porch with a locked door entry. Inside, there was a ledge around the top of the room, perfect for displaying all of Danny's little collectibles. It was carpeted and had its own ceiling fan!

Each room, except the kitchen, had a ceiling fan. The floors were hardwood and even though it was in need of upgrades and some repair work, it was undoubtedly a gift from God, and it was all ours …and the bank's. ("Except the Lord build the house, they labor in vain that build it: except the Lord keep the city, the watchman waketh but in vain." Psalm 127:1 KJV).

God had given us the home of our hearts and we would never forget to honor Him with praise and give our testimony to others about His goodness. We were blessed!

CHAPTER XI

Bleak Future: Look to the Son to Brighten Your Day

In 1996, Danny had applied for and was hired as a diesel truck mechanic, a job he had been doing all his life, but now he received benefits and higher pay. Everyone who knew Danny knew if they had any kind of mechanical problems, he was the man to see. Most of them were too poor to pay garage bills and usually each weekend was spent helping someone with their cars or trucks at his shop at our home. Many of his weekend customers were Christians who appreciated his talents, knowing he did all his work with integrity. He would help them any way he could when they needed him and toss in his testimony as an added bonus.

He listened to his gospel music radio stations as he worked and tuned in to all the preachers who encouraged him and ministered to him as he changed tires or changed oil or did brake jobs for his customers.

One of his favorite gospel singers was a local man, Forest Combs. He was also the pastor of a church called New Beginnings Christian Fellowship. A seed was planted in his little shop. Soon our spirits were aching to experience a more anointed worship service. ("Draw nigh to God, and He will draw nigh to you." James 4:8a KJV). We were trying to reach out to God. ("Humble yourselves in the sight of the Lord, and He shall lift you up." James 4:10 KJV).

God was definitely lifting us up and we felt the Spirit was leading us on a closer walk with Him. Just attending church wasn't enough. We were hungry for knowledge of this new life, and God was ready to feed us with His Word.

(September 1999) We left the Southside Baptist Church. We still had many friends who attended there but we never adapted well to the new church and I was still strongly drawn to the worship of the Pentecostal churches. I was afraid Danny would not want to change to a Pentecostal worship service even though I was sure he would enjoy the music.

I attended Sunday school at the Baptist church and then drove across town to the New Beginning Christian Fellowship Church to be a part of the worship service on the the first Sunday in September when Danny was scheduled to work. I figured I would just scout it out for us, to see if the Spirit was good there. I couldn't stop my praise for the service there.

The music was beautiful and the Spirit was powerful! I prayed Danny would receive the new church as I had. I needed the satisfaction of the Spirit-filled service, but never having attended a Pentecostal church, I feared Danny would not be as receptive as I was, however, he fit like he was born into the church and everybody welcomed us.

The pastor was a gospel singer who had recorded his music in Nashville and all the gospel music radio stations played his songs. He and his wife were both like celebrities and we were proud to be a part of their congregation. They were all like family!

We met Geneva, a sister in the church who prepared the bulletins along with the countless other jobs and responsibilities she handled quite proficiently, but she had a limited income and no one to help her with her emergencies.

Her car broke down and when she called Danny, he called around for her to find an affordable alternator. Unfortunately, none of the quotes were affordable for her social security budget. Danny went to a salvage yard and repaired her car using the alternator he bought for her.

While he repaired her car, Geneva and I visited and caught up on church news. Out of the corner of my eye, I saw something move under her sofa and I kept watching until I saw a little white dog inch out from her hiding place. It was a poodle, exactly like the one I had to have euthanized ten years ago. I was not ordinarily someone who could be termed a dog lover.

I was taught early on pets were not a necessary expense, and I was never considered a child worthy of such a luxury. My one and only experience as a child pet owner was when my Uncle Ray brought a mongrel pup to me. He let me keep it for a few months before he came back and saw the 'house' I had built for my 'Blackie.' I was six years old. Carrying his shotgun, he walked outside and fired two

shots, saying, "That dog wasn't worth the bullets it took to kill it."
After that, I was very careful about what I wished. I knew people
like us didn't get useless animals just to love.

Thirty years later, I cried as I buried a white poodle who followed
me everywhere until she went into a coma. The vet declared her
brain dead, so as the day ended, a tiny mound in the back yard was
the only evidence I had once had a little dog who loved me. Now,
this little poodle was watching me with those same incredible eyes
that searched for my heart.

Once I shared the story with Danny about how I buried my little
dog and told him I wished she was still alive to share her with him.
He said he wasn't really a dog lover. I knew exactly how he felt so
I didn't pursue it, but, he added, if I found such a dog again at the
'right' price, we could try and see how it worked out. Now those big
eyes in that furry body, quivering with excitement, were trying to
penetrate my heart. I could see God at work… again, as I heard my
friend say, "She really likes you! I wish you'd take her home with
you. My son is not a dog lover. He drinks and she's afraid of him. I
think she would be good company for you."

As I walked outside, carrying my new little blessing, Danny
regretted the words he spoke, promising me that 'if the price was
right' we could get a little poodle to take the place of the one I
lost. He started to shake his head no but he didn't have the heart to
disappoint me.

Instead, he spoke to Geneva and said, "Okay, we will take her but
if it doesn't work out, you will have to take her back." Smiling, she
said, "Thank you, Danny," and reminded him she would pay him the
following month once she received her next social security check.
He shook his head, "No, you gave her the poodle so you don't owe
me anything. BUT, if I have to send her back to you, you'll have to
take the dog back, right?" She agreed to the conditions but asked,
"Then how much will I owe you all together for the part and your
labor?" Danny just shrugged, saying, "No, if it doesn't work out,
you just take the poodle back, I'll take the loss, and you won't owe
me anything even then." That has been his mode of operations ever
since; whatever God lays on his heart is the fee for the work done.

Geneva will always have a special place in our hearts which
were enlarged by the New Beginnings congregation, and now an

event was about to take place we wanted to share with our new church family.

My daughter Patty had started calling me and told me she was getting married, and she wanted to have a church wedding. I was surprised! She had turned her back on God years ago and wanted nothing to do with my Christian life. Yet, God promised in His Word, ("Train up a child in the way he should go: and when he is old, he will not depart from it." Prov. 22:6 KJV).

Patty longed for her own daughters to be a part of this special day, but she knew she had paid a hard price for the life she had chosen. Three years ago, her maternal rights were taken from her by the state of Florida. She was called in to sign the official papers on her birthday, November 18th. Her four daughters had been placed in foster care until an adoptive couple could qualify to be their new parents. (My prior experiences disqualified me from raising my grandchildren. With a broken heart, I watched them disappear from my life. But I still serve a God of miraculous events and I am waiting to bring them back into my life where they belong.)

The little church never looked more lovely. The aisles were decorated with flower garlands, and her wedding was beautiful. My granddaughter, Sarah, was the flower girl. She walked slowly with her little basket to the altar. With a quick glance to her proud Daddy, (my son Jimmy), she continued her promenade with a bounce in her step.

I saw the smile that glowed from the bride as she watched her niece with her light blonde hair in curled ribbons and my heart was full! I thought of little Brandi, my oldest granddaughter I had raised for three years, and remembered brushing her golden hair and tying ribbons in her ponytails. Tears filled my eyes, both in joy and sadness as I longed for my lost grandchildren, Patty's daughters.

Patty looked like an angel in her wedding gown, carrying the bouquet I made for her. We had her reception in the fellowship hall after the wedding. I baked her wedding cake, complete with ivory roses, cascading over the tiers with beads and lace. Everything was beautiful.

The day was peaceful and He graced our celebration with His presence there. It was the only way to start a new life together. A daily walk with God, based in a Word- teaching church, was the only way to make it work, but she was not ready to commit to any daily relationship with the Lord.

God allowed us this day to store in our memories for hard times yet to come, for the life she shared with her new husband and his family was anything but holy. She was in for the worst battle of her life…one that threatened her eternal soul. She needed the unity of a worship service, the power of prayer in one accord, if she was going to survive the coming years.

I was having a problem with my worship service, too. Every Sunday was like a concert for country gospel but then…every Sunday was like a concert for country gospel. It was like having your favorite ice cream every day, then every meal…and then suddenly you started to crave roast beef and potatoes, or the 'Meat' of the Word.

When the Spirit of God tells your heart He wants you to move, nothing can or will satisfy you until you are following the Lord's will.

Pastor Combs loved everyone up to and following the days of his retirement from the ministry due to health reasons. He pastored and sang for many years with his wife, Betty, until God told him he had earned the right to rest.

His assistant pastor, (and one-time pastor of First Full Gospel Church), became the new pastor of the New Beginnings Fellowship. Pastor Ulis Taylor and his wife, Luellen, were old time holiness people, attuned to the voice of God. As in the days of Moses, this best explains God's plan. ("And Joshua, the son of Nun was full of the Spirit of wisdom; for Moses had laid his hands upon him: and the children of Israel hearkened unto him, and did as the Lord commanded Moses." Deut. 34:9 KJV). Ulis Taylor would be the new leader for New Beginnings.

I was becoming very ill and nothing or no one was going to satisfy me now. I was having a problem digesting food and getting weaker every day. I was turning jaundiced and soon even water was making me nauseous. I felt my physical body was dying but my spiritual self was begging for attention. I had a good prayer life. I didn't want to die but if death should come, I knew my soul was ready. I needed more spiritual food now for I knew there was a much deeper nourishment waiting for me…still searching for that Holy

Ground. It was so close, I could taste it. God already had a plan of action started.

Dr. P. John Kim was my family doctor for more than twenty years. He was my friend through many personal crisis and always was able to make me smile when he said in his best Korean/English language, "you are beautiful lady. Why you so sick? You are TOUGH!" Then he flashed his wide grin and warmly squeezed my hand, but this time, he looked at me intently and with tears in his eyes he said, "This is no good." He shook his head sadly and spoke slowly, "You have liver cancer and there is no cure."

CHAPTER XII

Crisis Brings Anxiety: Christ Peaceably Calms Your Storms

I could see the pain in his face as he delivered the ominous news to me. I came to the doctor alone that day, believing I would be treated with a shot or medication for just a severe stomach virus. I knew I could always trust Dr. Kim to take good care of me.

I stood there, hearing him speak and even tears wouldn't come. My body seemed to have gone into a mechanical mode as I said, "Well, what do I do now? What's the next step?" I could see how uncomfortable Dr. Kim was as he tried to tell me about the kinds of 'possibilities' the University of Florida was trying to create. Medical breakthroughs at Shands Cancer Research facilities and if the right doctor there would be willing to take me as a patient, then MAYBE I could have a chance… even if it was a slim one!

He referred me to Dr. Alan Hemming, a young doctor with an incredible mind and an attitude that stopped the bravest student intern in his or her tracks. He was so good at his job, he wasted no time on pampering or bedside manners. He was not willing to give any credit for his successes to anyone but himself…and that was when we came face to face. He entered the room with his professional stance and spoke to me as if I wasn't even there, almost reading the results aloud. He said, with a strong tone of conviction, "I will take your case. You will need liver surgery. It's necessary that the damaged section of the liver be separated from what's left of the healthy liver…I will…"

At that point, I stopped him and I sensed not many patients or students had ever dared stop this man in mid-sentence before. I said, "Just a minute. I didn't say you were going to do the operation yet." He was stunned. He asked, "What are you saying?" I repeated I hadn't agreed to it yet.

First, he had to tell me if he believed in God. I don't think anyone had ever made him as uncomfortable as he was then. He tried to find the right words to fit in his position but finally he just asked honestly, "What do you care if I believe in God?" I answered without hesitation, "Because when we are in the operating room, I will be unconscious due to the anesthesia so I won't be able to listen to God's voice so that leaves only you. And I need to know YOU will be listening for His guidance."

He knew by the sound of my voice this was a deal breaker. I knew he was very uncomfortable with the question so I gave him a moment to reply. "I guess there might be 'something' out there, somewhere, with power." I reached for the pen, giving him my permission for surgery, which seemed to surprise him. I answered his quizzical look by saying, "You may not realize it now, but what you just said is called mustard seed faith. God can work with that. You can do my surgery."

("...Verily I say unto you, If ye have faith as a grain of mustard seed, ye shall say unto this mountain, Remove hence to yonder place; and it shall remove; and nothing shall be impossible unto you." Matt. 17:20 KJV).

At that moment, the wheels were set into motion to show the miraculous works of God. A wire was inserted very cautiously into my liver which 'lassoed' the diseased part. With a precise snap, the wire was tightened to cut off the flow of blood to the area. The surgeon could then (with God's help) successfully remove the diseased section from the liver. It wasn't always a success story. In fact, there was a 75% chance I wouldn't make it through surgery, but for now, I was sent back home waiting for the blood supply to be cut off while I got sicker each day.

The night came that we were waiting for, when my condition had peaked. Danny and I had to travel the sixty miles to the emergency room through one of the worst storms of the year. I called the pastor at his home and he said, "Be careful, those roads are bad tonight."

In a way, those few words of caution broke the last tie I felt for our old church. I hung up the phone and called the First Full Gospel Church in Watertown, Florida where Danny and I had been visiting a few times. The services were full of Holy Ghost power and I needed a good portion of strength on that cold dark night. The pastor at First Full Gospel Church, Stanley Ellis, answered my call with six simple words, "Tell me what I can do." I told him to pray as

I was on my way to the hospital as we spoke. ("And He said unto me, My grace is sufficient for thee: for My strength is made perfect in weakness." 2 Corinth. 12:9a KJV).

I tried to see the roadway with the lightning bolts blasting the highway every couple of miles. Danny was praying hard and seated next to me in the passenger seat; he was paying a dear price for those younger days of carelessness, wishing he could take the wheel but knowing he would be breaking the law, driving without a license. So he prayed with all his might, tears filling his eyes, his voice breaking with each plea.

At three o'clock in the morning, I never expected to see the couple from that church waiting for us when we arrived at the emergency room. The prayer chain had been started and when Marshall and Linda Davis received the call, they left their house to meet us at the hospital so we wouldn't be alone.

That night, I met a young man in the emergency room with a greater need than I. My illness had placed my physical life in danger, but his spiritual well being was in real jeopardy. The clean cut young man was a doctor, and much too young to have such a cynical nature.

I told him how sorry I was to keep him out at that hour. He smiled and reassured me, "It's really not that bad for me. I work four ten-hour shifts and I'm off Friday through Sunday night." I said, "Wow, that's great! You never have to miss church on Sunday, then."

Danny had to work alternating shift work so we valued the Sundays when he was able to attend church with me. It never occurred to me someone willingly stayed away from God's house on Sunday.

He said, "I don't go to church at all anymore." I don't really know if the spark of embarrassment I felt was from his neglect of God's house, or my impertinence in prying into his personal life, but he must have felt my discomfort because he began to explain, "You see, I was raised in a strict Baptist home. We were such strong Baptists I even attended a Baptist school. I grew up learning all those childish Bible stories and when I got older, I accepted the fact the Bible was all make-believe and I never went back."

Danny heard his reasoning and said, "Oh, no!" He rolled his

eyes in amusement because he knew even as sick as I was, I wasn't about to let that go unanswered. I said a silent prayer God would help me say what he needed to hear. I was a little surprised, too, when I heard myself say, "Really?"

That spurred him on as he began to explain his conviction, "Well, for example, look at Noah's ark. According to the story, Noah built a ship that was large enough to house every animal species in the WORLD, and we're not even talking one of each! He took no less than two, plus he carried extra aboard ship to serve as sacrifices! That is no less than impossible, yet how many times are we are taught to blindly believe such ridiculous stories?"

He was shaking his head as he made his point but I spoke with the words the Lord gave to me. God was ready for his doubts, "I never thought of it quite like that. You are absolutely right! It would be 'humanly' impossible to get all those animals in there! It would take an absolute miracle to get Noah's ark to truly exist. Anything else and it could never be possible." Smugly, he started to accept he had convinced me, then he just stopped and for a split second he winced and said, "Yes…I guess it would." I watched as he walked away humbly and I never saw him again. Yet I believe God gave him a reason to believe in miracles that night. My miracles were just beginning.

I sensed this was a crucial segment of my journey in my search for Holy Ground. We became members of the First Full Gospel Church, whose Father was and is a Holy God. Together, we faced many emergencies and life changing experiences.

The Davis family became our angels of mercy, at our beck and call at any hour of the day or night. If we called them, they responded with a smile and the Word. Praise God for brothers and sisters in the Lord who step out without question to minister to those in need!

CHAPTER XIII

Fear: Disease of Faith Deficiency; The Cure: Fervent Dose of Prayer

(December 10ᵗʰ, 2002) Church members and my family were gathered at the hospital as they received the details of my surgery. They were allowed to come early to say our final farewells, in case of my death, but I never heard anyone talk as though I wouldn't survive. A circle of faith was formed around me and the sincere, fervent prayers went out to an all powerful God. A miracle was the only acceptable answer for this group of prayer warriors, and a miracle was what we received.

The doubting surgeon was amazed. He had predicted my chances were slight, and even then, the next step would be the extended stay in the Intensive Care Unit... if I survived again. Then I was facing a long stay on the liver transplant floor (even though a transplant was never considered. Dr. Hemming said it wasn't a viable option for me). Again, my survival rate was minimal. Then the next couple of years would be spent in convalescent care at a nursing home or in convalescent care, if we followed the full medical agenda set out for me.

However, God had a plan that superseded the greatest surgical minds. Following a twelve and a half hour operation, I was brought into the ICU as planned, but from that time, a whirl of miracles was activated.

I had gone from the ICU to the liver transplant floor critical care ward, but only stayed there for two hours. I was receiving breathing treatments and at my appointed time for the next treatment, the technician entered with the brightest smile I had ever seen. I felt the joy of the Lord around him as he opened the door like an angel. "Knock, knock," he said, "breathing treatment!"

I motioned to him and asked cautiously, "Will it interfere with your schedule, if I delay it for a few minutes? This lady would like to ask me something about the Lord and heaven." He quickly responded by saying, "No, Ma'am, it sure won't. I'm sure you don't need any more treatments. Go on and have your talk and when you're done, we'll be moving you out of critical care to a room out there."

I thanked him and asked her, "Sister, do you have a question for me?" A frail hand appeared from the next bed as she said, "God sent you to me, that much I know. I've been troubled about my soul." I told her, "I feel in my spirit you have already made your peace with God. What more can I tell you?" She weakly smiled, as she told me, "I'm ninety-two years old and I am going to heaven tonight. I've made those plans long ago, but what I don't know is what happens when the body dies?"

I closed my eyes and prayed, "My Father, I come to Your throne, to find peace for the soul of my sister in this room. I ask You right now, Lord, to use this humble vessel to speak Your words of comfort and understanding to her as she prepares herself to leave this world." I knew I was no authority on such matters, (I not only didn't have all the right answers, I didn't even know all the questions!) but the Spirit was prepared to answer her with wisdom and truth. As I spoke, I heard the words, but it was from the Lord, for I serve a living God who desires to give His children every provision for any need:

("Therefore, we are always confident, knowing that, whilst we are at home in the body, we are absent from the Lord: {For we walk by faith, not by sight:} We are confident, I say, and willing rather to be absent from the body, and to be present with the Lord." 2 Corinth. 5:6-8 KJV). I raised my hands to illustrate to her, "Absent in the body," and I folded my hands in prayer, quickly releasing them, and lifting them high into the air to praise the Lord, "Present with the Lord." I heard her sigh peaceably.

I smiled my 'thank You' to God, when she asked me again, "Will I know my family when I get to heaven?" I needed only to remind her when Stephen was stoned to death, he looked into heaven and saw Jesus standing at the right hand of God. If we had no recollection of our earthly body, how could he know this was Jesus he had seen? (Acts 7:55-56 KJV).

The door to our hospital room opened as she closed her eyes. The attendant who entered the room said, "Miss Helen? You are being moved to a semi-private room tonight. Are you ready to go?"

I nodded. Yes, I was ready to go now, for God had used this injured vessel one more time, and I was basking in that blessing. That night, one beautiful lady celebrated her homegoing and I settled into my next step of my journey.

From the time I came out of surgery, several visitors to my bedside had asked me to pray for them in their times of duress, either from damaged relationships or illnesses. I can still hear their desperate pleas, "Are you the lady who prays?" and "Will you pray for me?" I never turned anyone away, but I sometimes lapsed back into my medicated sleep before they left.

As I gained strength, I counted twenty-seven times I was asked to pray for others during my two week stay in the hospital. God is so wonderful!

Linda Davis and her husband, Marshall, came to our home daily, where Linda instructed home-care nurses how to dress my wounds.

I had an incision, two inches deep, two inches wide and it spanned thirty-two inches, snaking the outer part of my rib cage. Most of the nurses had never seen such a post-operative condition. Many had to excuse themselves as they became sickened by the trench that was carved into my body, but not Linda! She just cleaned, bandaged and suctioned the area. When the liver pump that was used to suction out the infectious fluids shut down at 2 a.m., she helped us without wavering.

Marshall was Danny's life support and spiritual mentor so we were truly blessed with our 'angels of mercy.' The church women cooked for us every day. I never missed a test or any doctor's appointment. Someone was always available for my needs.

When January 24th, 2003 arrived, Marshall and Linda took us to see Dr. Hemming for my first follow-up appointment. The liver pump was removed that day and a surgeon was speechless as he looked at me in awe. I smiled and said, "You do good work, Doc!" "Not me!" he replied, as he pointed to heaven and smiled.

Some who hear my testimony believe the conversion of Dr. Hemming was the reason for my cancer, but I know God does not give cancer. Cancer is a disease out of the pits of hell. It destroys lives and families and finances and confidence, but Christ is bigger than cancer. His healing power overcame the curse. He came that we might have life and have it MORE ABUNDANTLY! That is NOT a definition of cancer. Some will survive it and some won't. Why? I can't answer that, but I do know what made me strong in the days and nights of physical weakness when I appeared to be dying... God. Am I a fanatic? Absolutely! I am entirely sold out because He has given me life, a new life with all the blessings! I like to explain this in a way so anyone with even an ounce of logic can understand it to overcome their doubts:

I do know the human body is just a vessel through which the spirit flows, and when that vessel is destroyed through age or disease or injury, the spirit will still survive. I also know the condition of the man's spirit is of greater importance to God than the temporary physical body, for the body was created to return to dust but the spirit goes further, either into eternal glory or eternal hell.

I know this. I have seen lives changed when men and women accept this fact. If God says something, He means it. His promises are steadfast. His rules are on the mark, but He lets you choose if you want to follow the road to hell or be obedient and follow God and His plan for your life, which leads to eternal life.

When the right choice is made, you become a child of favor, for your Father is the King. As a favored child, He sends you directions and rules and helpers along the way so your life can be blessed with many advantages. He teaches lessons we sometimes don't understand, but even the lessons are gifts! One very important gift is the Bible, His book of promises. He teaches how to live a blessed and favored life, but this doesn't change the fact that our bodies are still flesh and imperfect. Eventually, all flesh must die. Eternal life is only available when we get to the other side, but there is no reason for man to accept pain and agony. When we truly seek spiritual truth through studying God's Word, and desire a close walk with Him, then our eyes are opened and we see...actually SEE what 'Thus saith the Lord.' We awaken to a new understanding of God's power, to overcome pain and fear. Sweet peace can fill our bodies despite disease.

During my illness, it was nearly impossible for me to digest food, and I was too weak to even go to the bathroom without someone practically carrying me. With the physical eyes, I'm sure many had given up on my recovery, but I had Danny post the names of Jesus up on the wall where I could see them clearly, so even when I couldn't hold my Bible I could still praise Him … Wonderful Counselor … My Rock and My Salvation… I needed that strength, because all the drugs on earth were not designed to take away the pain I should have suffered, but when I reached the Spiritual altitude of praise, I knew He was in control and everything was going to be okay. Was I pain-free? No, but I was fear-free. Danny and I learned a lot about 'leaning on Jesus.' We felt blessed to be a part of an incredibly strong, and loving church family, but there was one missing piece: my daughter was still my biggest heartache.

She had been supportive throughout my hospitalization. Many times she said she prayed for me. I knew my daughter loved me, but she wouldn't come close to me. She knew my faith but she had not accepted Christ in her own life. One day I went to the altar to pray, I wrote 'Patricia Lynn' on a piece of paper and laid it on the altar. I said, "I am trusting her in Your care, Father." Then I walked away. I was not prepared for the events that followed, but Danny and I faced them together. With God's help, we survived. If you are struggling with impossible situations, let go! Let God have it. ("Take My yoke upon you, and learn of me; for I am meek and lowly in heart: and ye shall find rest unto your souls." Matthew 11:29 KJV).

CHAPTER XIV

What is Life? Sands in Time, Waiting for the Rushing Tide

(Saturday, May 3rd, 2003) A phone call stopped the beating of my heart. I could hear the words being spoken, but I couldn't accept it. Danny had called me on my cell phone and told me to come home right away. He adamantly refused to tell me the urgency but now as I sat in the quiet stillness of my home, I heard each word like a stab in my heart. "Patty's gone, Honey. Cleve just called. She died of a heart attack this morning. It was very sudden."

He was holding me in his arms and I was grateful as my legs began to weaken. He guided me to the sofa as he said, "She had been to the doctor for chest pains but he said it was just stress from the physical requirements of her job."

She was a manager in a convenience store and she was always lifting boxes and straining muscles, but this was the first time she had sought a doctor's help. He gave her a shot for the pain and sent her back to work the next day. As she drove onto the bridge in Port St. Lucie where she lived with her husband, Cleve, and his family, she sensed there was something very wrong.

She was found with her cell phone in her hand as she was trying to make a call to her husband during the last moments of her life. For two hours, her car was passed by several onlookers who had no time to stop.

Finally, a co-worker noticed and stopped to check on her on his way to the store where he worked with her. She never regained consciousness. My little girl was dead. I would never see her again!

A big part of my heart froze that day and I called out to God. I didn't understand. I knew we had an agreement! How could this happen? Children were not supposed to die before the parents! We were old and our children had so much more life to live!

There had to be some mistake, but I knew there was no mistake.

I felt like an old crumpled rag and I needed to be consoled, but Danny was crying with me. Even when he held me, it just wasn't enough. I needed my Father. I needed to be in my Father's House.

That evening the church was having a gospel sing and worship service and we had planned to go, but that was before I had received my devastating news. Danny gently held me and tried to offer words of comfort.

Still sobbing, I tried to speak, "Tonight…" He just held me out from him and said, "Baby, forget about the sing tonight. Why don't you just go lie down and I'll make some calls for you, okay? Everyone will understand if we don't go tonight. I'll stay right here with you. I promise."

He didn't understand at that moment I wanted to go to the sing that night. No, I NEEDED to go to the sing that night. I had to be in my Father's house, at the same altar where I left my daughter in His care. As I told Danny, he accepted my decision but said, "If you need to leave early, we can. It's your call."

I got dressed for the service that night without thinking. All my actions seemed mechanical, just going through the motions. We left the house solemnly. As we saw the church come into view, I swallowed the big lump in my throat and said, "Danny, do you think God had the time to offer her one last chance to get saved?" It would be just so unbearable to think of Patty not getting saved before she died. He held my hand and tried to comfort me, "We probably will never know that." I told him, "I placed her on the altar and left her in His care. I can't believe He didn't reach her in time."

I wiped my tears and went inside where the music and praising was already started. Standing on the platform was a pretty, petite woman who was reaching for the microphone. She looked out over the congregation and I heard her say, "Is there a Sister Helen here tonight?" She had never met me, but she had heard through the prayer lines I had just been through a battle with cancer.

She smiled as she said, "Jesus wants me to sing this song just for you, Sister." Tonya O'Neal sang these words softly, "I saw your tears; I heard you cry. She is here… with Me." Then, she looked confused as she turned around and looked back to the other six musicians on the platform and started singing a different song altogether.

I never heard those words before in any song, nor have I heard them since, but I am convinced it was a message of confirmation from God that He honored His covenant with me. My daughter was now at peace, with no more suffering or abuse.

That night, I asked Pastor Stan Ellis if I could say a word to the people. He said, "You sure can!" I stood there at the microphone, and told the congregation how I had just received word my daughter had died.

I told how she was running from God and she no longer trusted the church. She lived in a world of sin because she was damaged in a world where a preacher father could abuse her physically and sexually. She only felt safe outside in the world when she should have been lifted up and protected by children of God. She lived in an upside down world of misfits and drugs, sin and neglect.

Yet God treasured her. He proved it at the last moments of her life when He came to her and carried her safely home. He knew her life was too hard. Her new family was not of God and she was daily consumed by satanic influences. There was hardly a chance for her to become a new child of God. She would just go back to the family she married into and be surrounded by evil. So as she waited for death that day on the bridge, she was welcomed into the kingdom of God. She was finally safe at home in heaven.

I asked if anyone in the sanctuary had any doubts where they would spend their eternity, would they please come to the altar and talk to their Father. We are not promised tomorrows. Patty was thirty-two. She was healthy and had her whole life ahead of her, but God knew He had to bring her home in His time.

If you are reading this, think about it. If you were the one, found on the bridge, would you be entering heaven's gates, or hell's fury? Don't wonder. Make a point to set the record straight. Know this day it is well with your soul, for tomorrow comes quickly and we don't know what evils it may bring.

The altar was full that night, but your altar can be anywhere you meet with God. He always waits for you at His altar. Talk with Him and know you are a child of God.

The next few days were a time of anguish as I prepared to go to my daughter's funeral… the final good-bye my son-in-law and his family totally controlled. I was told not to come. She was a part of their family now and I was dismissed as though we had been just passing acquaintances. Surely, the grief I had suffered had impaired my understanding. So I wiped my tears and asked my son-in-law to call back and speak to Danny about the funeral arrangements. I waited for his call but it didn't come.

The house was quiet since I was told my daughter was gone. I wanted to go to the hospital where she was taken in an unconscious state, but no one would tell me where she had been taken. Within hours, she was in the hands of the coroner who had to perform an autopsy.

I called the county where the coroner's office was located, but I was told all the details had been sealed by the next of kin, her husband. When would I be told about the visitation? The secretary told me I had to ask the husband, due to the privacy law. Where would the funeral services be held? Ask the husband. Where was the cemetery? Ask the husband. This was so bizarre! I never would have ever believed my son-in-law, Cleve would shut me out.

Patty and I had recently made exciting progress in our relationship. She had just called me the week before to tell me she had been saying prayers to God to watch over me since my cancer was found. I was so thrilled to hear her speak freely of praying. God was really showing me evidence of His covenant with me to save my household. Now she was gone and I couldn't even see her as she was laid to rest. I was not about to take no for an answer.

I called Patty's home and as I heard Cleve's voice, I recognized the sorrow we shared. "Cleve, this is Helen. Is there anything I can do to help you through this?" He said, "She's gone and no one can do anything."

I knew how hopeless he felt, but I couldn't console him any further, so Danny took the telephone from me. His voice was full of compassion as he said, "Hello, Cleve. Helen is taking this really hard. Isn't there some way we can do this together to lighten the pain for all of us? Why don't you let us take care of Patty's arrangements here where her family and friends are. We'll pay for all the expenses."

Cleve spoke quietly explaining his family was making all the decisions, but Danny tried one more time, "Patty was Helen's daughter, Cleve. She needs to do a little something to help. We don't doubt you will do right by her. You love her, but Cleve, you're twenty-three. It may be years from now, but you will probably marry again. Let us do this for Patty, ok? Her mother and her brothers are here. Won't you please let us bring her back home to lay her to rest?"

Cleve said firmly, "My family wants her here." Danny hurriedly tried to ask him to at least tell us where the funeral would be but Cleve hung up the phone without saying good-bye. I felt limp... with no answers and no peace. ("He maketh the storm a calm, so that the waves thereof are still." Psalm 107:29 KJV). "Lord," I prayed, "send Your calm to my spirit, for I am tossed in this storm and I'm so very tired of the struggle." I curled into a ball on the couch by the telephone and I slept peaceably for the first time in days.

The telephone jarred my senses and I jumped to grab the receiver, "Mrs. Hill? I'm sorry to disturb you but I've had second thoughts about our discussion yesterday." It was the secretary at the coroner's office. "I realize I could lose my job, but I couldn't stop thinking about what you're going through. I am not allowed to give you any details about the funeral arrangements, but if you could follow my directions, you might be able to get your answers there. In fact, the Best Western Hotel across from a local funeral home may have a room where you can stay for a couple of days." Before I could thank her appropriately, she hung up.

With her directions, my family started the drive to Port St. Lucie. As I opened the door of the funeral home, I stopped to take a deep breath and I knew something wasn't right. Something was missing … flowers! There were no flowers…no music. There was just a small coffin that held the body of my beautiful daughter, dressed in her wedding gown complete with a small bouquet for her carefully placed hands. A chair had been placed at the head of the coffin and the director steered me to the seat, telling me it was just customary for the mother to be escorted there. There should never be a custom for a mother's seat at her child's funeral. Children were not supposed to die this young!

I turned to look at Danny. This was all too new for me. I wanted to be close to him through this ordeal. As we entered the alcove designated for the family, we were quickly confronted by Cleve's grandmother who informed me we weren't welcome there. She hurried to the honored seat and sat down with determination. The funeral director tried to apologize but I assured him seating was not an issue about which I cared. I assured him my little girl was with Jesus, not in that box they all huddled around like scavengers.

I stood beside my daughter's coffin and remembered her laughter and the way she sounded when she answered the phone. My heart was breaking.("Forsake me not, O Lord: O my God, be not far from me." Psalm 38:21 KJV).

The memory of a song kept me going; the lyrics were precious to me. "I saw your tears; I heard you cry. She is here ... with Me." Now Jesus was carrying me through this incredibly deep, dark valley. What I wouldn't give to have had one last day with her to hear her tell me how she got saved.

I knew somewhere within her heart there was a remembrance of her knowing God. She loved to sing the song, 'He Lives.' I smiled as I remembered her older brother, Jimmy begging me, "Mom, can't you make her stop?" His sister loved to sing about serving a risen savior, but Jimmy was right. It was almost painful to hear how off-key she sang. I said softly, "Sing now, Baby Girl. Jesus wants to hear you sing!" ("Sing unto the Lord, O ye saints of His, and give thanks at the remembrance of His holiness." Psalm 30:4 KJV). Someday my little girl would be waiting at the gates of heaven with a sweet smile of victory and a song she learned from the angels!

I had my confirmation from God and it was going to take every ounce of that to get me through the graveside service the following day.

Cleve and his family had decided not to tell us where the cemetery was located. In fact, they came to inform us a limousine was going to take his family to the site but we were not included.

The next day we went to the funeral home and waited for the hearse to go to the cemetery so we could follow the driver. We darted in and out of traffic trying quickly to predict the lane changes and turns on the route. Soon the hearse entered a cemetery and we followed.

The canopy had been erected and the casket was in place when I saw the funeral director again motion me to a seat at the front of the rows of chairs designated for the family. Again, the grandmother took the seat. My heart went out to the elderly man on the front row, Cleve's grandfather. He obviously loved my daughter very much.

She had a special place in her heart for elderly people. I guess her heart was just reserved for strangers who needed her. She took in strays constantly. Sometimes the strays were dogs and cats and sometimes they were homeless people who sensed her gigantic heart. I worried that some day she might bring home a serial killer, but one thing was sure, her life was never dull.

When you knocked on her door, you never knew who would answer or how many blankets you would have to step over on her living room floor. Inside those blankets was anyone from a sick child to a smelly, homeless man down on his luck. I tried for years to teach her the difference between having acquaintances and the complete opposite end of the spectrum, that place you reserved for best friends you could really trust with life and death issues. To Patty, there was no difference, but where I came from, one learned to be cautious. In Patty's world, she just loved everybody equally. Maybe she had much more wisdom than Mom, but I believe possibly, my prayers built a wall of protection all around her in her innocence.

The old man sat sobbing before me this day. He was blessed for having known my daughter, yet broken by his loss, as he cried, "Why did God take her? She was all I had left." Together, we cried and grieved while I told him God said she was in heaven waiting to welcome us home some day. I hugged him and he smiled weakly.

A clergyman stood next to the casket and said, "We come into this world and do the best we can and then we die. Today we are laying Patricia to rest. Her time is over." As he just walked away, I looked around in disbelief!

For thirty two years, my daughter filled our lives and this was how she was to be remembered? I glanced at the Director and he saw my discomfiture. He came to me and said, "I'm sorry. The husband requested that no one be allowed to speak."

I swallowed hard and asked Him, "Couldn't I just say something for my daughter? It's all I have now." He thought about it for an instant and said, "Go on, Mother, I'll deal with the consequences later."

I laid my hand slowly down on the cold steel of the blue capsule that held my child's lifeless body and said, "I know we all came here today to see Patty one more time, but, you see, that isn't possible. What you see here is a container that holds the earthly vessel we named Patricia Lynn. But her spirit still lives."

"She became a child of God recently and her name is written down in the Lamb's Book of Life. Some day I will walk with her again... in heaven. I know this is true because God had a covenant with me where He promised my household would be saved. On the day I received word from man that Patty had passed away, my heavenly Father assured me He welcomed her home."

"I know Patty would be honored if I asked you, her friends and family, to take a moment of silence, not to mourn her death, but to search your hearts. If you had been the driver they found on the bridge, who lost her life, would you be celebrating your spiritual homecoming, or would you be entering a sinner's eternity in hell?"

A group of young men and women had arrived at the cemetery in the limousine, following a night of drinking and partying. They were all suffering hangovers mixed with their grief but my words were affecting them. Suddenly, they were sitting quietly in their seats, heads bowed and I sensed each friend was seriously questioning the condition of their soul.

I turned and my husband smiled at me with love and support. We started to walk away when I saw Patty's mother-in-law blocking my way. She was a foreboding figure, nearly six feet tall and a huge frame. She forcefully grabbed my wrist and her vice-like grip held me captive. I stood there waiting for her to speak. I was surprised by the tones of the voice that came from her. "Your daughter was never saved! She was with me for two weeks and she belonged to me!" I knew this was not the confrontation of a grieving woman. I recognized the evil that stood there before me and I was not swayed. ("Submit yourselves therefore to God. Resist the devil, and he will flee from you." James 4:7 KJV).

As I stood there, Danny put his arm around me for support. My body was still weak from the cancer surgery I had undergone a few months ago, but my spirit surged! I said, "My daughter was taught early about Jesus Christ and how He shed His blood for her salvation. God confirmed she was saved before she died...AND YOU CAN'T DO A THING ABOUT IT. NOW GET OUT OF MY WAY!" The woman was startled and jumped away from me as if I had thrown scalding water on her. I will always believe she was overpowered by the Spirit of God!

As I sat in our car for the return trip home, I knew the days ahead would be very difficult. How does one ever recover from placing their child's body in a cold grave? I had to keep reminding myself 'she's not there.'

CHAPTER XV

Weary Traveler: Rest Beneath His Wings And Rise With Him

For all the miracles I had seen, the power of God I had witnessed and all the prayers I had seen answered, it seemed unbelievable I would question anything about God. I've heard others say, "Don't get too comfortable on the mountaintop; it's just a pit stop before you careen into the valleys of despair."

I wondered how anyone who was a child of God could take on such a pessimistic attitude, but now in my solitude, I questioned God, 'Why must my spirit be so heavy? What are you trying to teach me? How can I remain strong, when I keep getting knocked off my feet? I don't know where to turn or where to go! I have never felt so lost. You said You would never leave me nor forsake me; yet I search for You and I can't hear Your voice. I read Your Word; I don't understand! How can I walk this journey of life if You are not guiding me?'

Visitors came to comfort me for my loss and despite their best intentions, their words were hollow sounds. "God is in control. He had a reason to take Patty home;" but the worst of all was, "Sometimes we try to be good mothers by praying for our children. Maybe it's time we just march into their lives and take a stand so they don't get into all that trouble, and we wouldn't have to be burying our children." 'God, was prayer not enough? Had I failed Patty? Is it my fault she died? Could I have changed the events in her life if I had been more assertive? Dear God, did I kill my daughter by my neglect? Have I repeatedly failed her until You had to rescue her… from me?'

All the way home, my head was spinning from the agony of my thoughts. I had to get to the church. I knew God didn't live there, that He is everywhere, wherever we are, but there was a holy ambience there and it was truly my sanctuary.

As I entered the building, I felt as if I had never been there before.

Something had changed. I walked to the pew I always share with Danny and looked around. This church was the place where prayers were answered; the altars were stained with the tears of the saints of bygone generations. I rose and walked to the communion table near the altar and noticed the vial of oil that was used in prayers for healing broken bodies and diseases…and lost souls.

As I turned, I suddenly felt a strong presence and I recognized the power that engulfed me there. I removed my shoes for I sensed I was standing on Holy Ground. I lifted my hands to praise Him. In the distance I heard the lonesome wail of the CSX train barreling down the tracks across the road from the Church. I walked outside and saw the train was approaching, and the wailing came one more time. I wondered, 'Lord, have I reached the destination You had planned for me? What was Your purpose for me in this place? There must be more to this journey!'

I was no longer that little seven year old girl, nestled in that shanty with my sister. I had been out on the front lines of spiritual wars and conquered the enemy. The victory was mine and yet I knew that in my own strength, I had accomplished nothing. ("For we are His workmanship, created in Jesus Christ unto good works, which God hath before ordained that we should walk in them." Ephesians 2:10 KJV). Now He had another pathway laid out before me.

I was standing on Holy Ground that few people had ever reached in a lifetime, but how could I lead others to this inner sanctum? This was a spiritual journey unlike anything I had ever faced. All my life I had followed wherever He led in my search for Holy Ground, but what message was He sending out to His children to lead them to this Promised Land? What an awesome responsibility He had handed to me! This was an urgent pilgrimage. I knew I had to find the root of His covenant here, but where did I start? "In the beginning… God…" Once again I heard His voice leading me and assuring me He would walk alongside me through my journey, and once again, I wasn't really sure of my destination, just my Guide.

I left the sanctuary as I felt drawn to the entry door. How many lost souls had come through those doors, never to be the same again? The old sinner man was left at that tear-stained altar and a new man was filled with the Spirit, washed in the Blood from that old cross of Calvary. As he steps out of these hallowed walls, he knows a new strength he has within him, a purpose to share the Word, and the wisdom to pursue his calling.

As if being summoned, the tracks were rumbling, the whistle piercing the evening sky and my messenger train roared by. "What is it about trains, Lord, that You tug on my heartstrings and make me reminisce?" I wanted so desperately for Him to open my eyes to this calling He had given me, instead of my memory of bygone days and the reality of my search for Holy Ground. "I have searched  for years for Your Holy Presence. I know You have shown me so many signs of Your nature and yet I feel as if I am searching for the wind! I feel the breeze, I hear the gentlest whisper, and all creation is moved by Your touch, but I have not seen the face of the force, only the effects, which are mighty and so plentiful! How I long to shout it out to this generation of indifferent children! You are worthy to be praised! You need to be praised! God, I behold Your Glory, but I have only touched the surface of Your Spirit! I must go deeper with You, for You are my breath and my life and without Your favor, I am nothing! My life is but a form, whose orbit was created by Your Power. I am only empowered by Your Word which birthed my existence. Now, Father, I come before You to seek Your wisdom, that I may take my journey with passion, for You have prepared this walk for me."

I stood and turned to face the podium. I touched the sacred altar where countless appeals were made to the sinner man, "Come to Jesus, before it's too late! He's at the door of your heart, knocking, asking you to let Him come in, but only you can open it. All I can do for you is give you the invitation to the cross, where you can lay down your burdens and sin-stained heart; where you can repent and be born again, be freely forgiven, fully restored. Won't you come?" I could see saints of old, standing all over the house of God, tears streaming down their faces as loved ones came down to the altar. This was the beginning of a blood-bought covenant for each of them! A promise from God! They would be His people and He would be their God, forever! The pianist was playing softly, 'Just As I Am.' The voices sweetly sang, "Just as I am, without one plea, but that Thy blood was shed for me, and that Thou bidd'st me come to Thee, O Lamb of God, I come! I come!" A sacred lull fell over the congregation.

The pianist knows to allow God to direct the flow of music; the tempo, the keys, touched by the Holy Ghost. The pastor is John Dortch. The pianist is his son, Robert. I am awed by the presence. God's covenant is proven once more, as a Christian father serving God, smiles at his son who was received into the Lamb's Book of Life. I knew households were being saved, protected by the Spirit, walking in the covenant!

Another young pianist, sitting in the pew, watches her cousin play the music for the congregation. Joyce Dortch knows about sinners coming to God! Her Uncle John was a Pentecostal man of God who pulled no punches. He knew a higher authority to whom he answered for the souls he encountered. Joyce was taught to seek after things of God, that the world offered no benefit for her soul.

Worshippers looked around the room in the small wooden church (constructed from the remnants of two sawmill houses) and tried to reposition themselves on the benches, to prevent the pinch by the planks of wood that served as seating. Those seats were a part of the church's history. One member after another reminisced how their clothes got snagged or legs pinched by the rough-hewn seats, but it never hindered the old time preaching. They continued long into the night, to

Inside Old Wooden Church

a congregation who hated to leave the fervent sermons and those anointed services!

The members were poor, hard-working holiness people. There was no money for padded pews and carpeted floors. There was no air conditioning. Someone said, "Our church was prayer conditioned, and that was good enough!" They were satisfied with the church they built, and they were blessed! Just then, the Atlantic Seaboard came barreling down the tracks. As the windows rattled, one of the men moved to the pane of glass, holding it in place, until the train faded away.

The window pane was probably held by a deacon, William Henry Westberry, born October 27, 1866. He married Mamie Murray on December 10, 1911. Pictured here are W. H. Westberry, wife, Mamie, and son, Thomas H. Westberry, born on October 26, 1913. Mamie was born in 1896 and died at the age of 25, in 1921. God blessed this man with three children. Thomas, (infant son in picture) was married to Hilda Harrington but had no children. Niron (Buck) Westberry and wife, Edith Tanner had one daughter, Sandra. W.H. Westberry's daughter, Allie Mae Westberry, had a daughter, Charlotte (Spann)Trowell and a son, Gary Frank Spann. Gary followed in the steps of his grandfather, accepted the position of deacon of his local church in Georgia, and served for many years

The Westberry Family

until he went to be with the Lord on July 2nd, 2007. ("Lo, children are an heritage of the Lord: and the fruit of the womb is his reward. As arrows are in the hand of a mighty man; so are children of the youth. Happy is the man that hath his quiver full of them: they shall not be ashamed, but they shall speak with the enemies in the gate." Psalm 127:3-5 KJV).

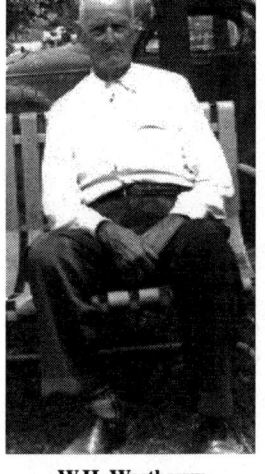

He left a legacy for all, (pictured here in his early 90s), and joined his ancestors with the Lord on November 25, 1960. He will be remembered, historically, for the part he played in the land purchased by the church as one of three trustees named in the original document:

"On the 30th day of August, A.D. 1941, Adele Dees, single, of the County of Columbia, State of Florida confirmed and granted the deed to the land recognized as Lot of Block 'A' in the town of Watertown to the Trustees of the Watertown Congregational Holiness

W.H. Westberry

Church, W. H. Westberry, J. C. Padgett, and George Church, and their successors, for the sum of Forty and no/100 dollars, sealed and filed on this date, August 30th, 1941." Amen. The seed was sown! ("Ye are the children of the prophets, and of the covenant which God made with our fathers, saying unto Abraham, 'And in thy seed shall all the kindreds of the earth be blessed.'" Acts 3:25 KJV). The God of father Abraham had big plans for His children. For over two thousand years, men of faith stood on the faith of the covenant made between Abraham and the one true God, Jehovah! The God of Abraham has big plans for His children who serve Him today, too. God is the same yesterday, and today and forever, and your name doesn't have to be Abraham. God gave His Son to the world as the unblemished sacrifice for our sins. Each generation needs to be told of the covenant God has made with His people, of the fulfilled promises, of battles fought and won, of bodies healed and families restored! His covenant is offered freely to all. If you will become His people, He will become your God. His blessing will be for you and all the generations of your household! It is Holy Ground! I turned aside as I left the old saints to follow the leading of the Spirit as I continued to search for Holy Ground.

CHAPTER XVI

Yesterdays Are Gateways To the Promises of Tomorrow's Dreams

He brought me to this little church, to lead me to His higher purpose. ("For I would that ye knew what great conflict I have for you, and for them at Laodicea, and for as many as have not seen my face in the flesh; That their hearts might be comforted, being knit together in love, and unto all riches of the full assurance of understanding, to the acknowledgement of the mystery of God, and of the Father and of Christ; In whom are hid all the treasures of wisdom and knowledge." Col. 2:1-3 KJV). The congregation of believers were being prepared for higher things and I was anxious to join in the quest for this treasure!

God was concerned that many were weak because they had never actually seen the living Jesus Christ, so He wanted them to use their talents, as a group of people 'knit together' to grow into a new relationship with Him, depending on one another for the strength to establish a good life based on knowing… with a deep, searching desire to understand …the miraculous love of our Heavenly Father for His children! This was a new level of my search for Holy Ground! Who were these people who won the heart of God? From where did they come and how were they formed? I needed to know!

I asked God to open doors for me that I might learn of this place where the Spirit dwells so richly. Early morning hours found me pouring over web sites and stories in old newspapers. Books, magazines, museums, historical studies were scheduled weekly. No stone was unturned! Telephone calls and letters, e-mails and reunions offered the answers for which I searched, piece by piece. If God ordained this search for me, I was not going to be a disappointment to Him. Those saints of old must be a key to my passage!

At that point, it had not occurred to me there was not one piece of information needed by God. He already had all the answers! After months of praying incessantly, fasting weekly, and absorbing His

Word for no less than two hours a day, I finally started to understand. He was trying all this time to hold my attention! He just wants quality time with His children, not just at the meal time blessing or crisis comforting. We have been adopted into the family of the chosen children of God; we need to get acquainted with our Father! He is not an absentee parent or a deadbeat dad! So get used to Him being a big part of your life, your home, your friends and activities! He was even helping me to see the old Watertown and understand its' connection to my search for Holy Ground!

Watertown was a community formed in the company town built by Alexander Gunn Paul in approximately 1880. Mr. Paul named the town for Watertown, Wisconsin, where he was born. Mr. Paul provided housing at low rents, and even established the necessary companies for the unincorporated town to exist as a community.

These businesses included a bank, a commissary, a bottling plant, a hotel, an ice plant and an elementary school. Rumors have said there was even a hospital, but I found no proof of this. Some believe the hospital was located in Alligator, later called Lake City, Florida.

Watertown, today, is relatively unknown. The community lies 60 miles south of Jacksonville, Florida. Area businesses use Lake City addresses, city services, and have postal affiliation with the larger town. However, in 1915, the little town started booming!

The East Coast Lumber Company was the 2nd largest in Florida and families were planning for the future. A.E. Paul was the company president who recently moved to Florida from Wisconsin in the first decade of the new century. A.G. Paul tossed the gauntlet to the younger man, A. E. Paul,  **Commissary Tokens** and taught him the duties he inherited. East Coast Lumber Company of Watertown became the 2nd largest in the south! Watertown was on the map! The lumber company started issuing their own scrip. Coins were made of an alloy of tin, copper and 25% silver and used in the Commissary for clothes or any other necessities for the men and women who were employed by the Paul businesses. Bold headlines in the 1919 Citizen Reporter blasted in a full page ad: "Watertown

Owners of Smith Store Ready For Business

Trading Company, The Big Store of Columbia County," but the popular place to go was Smith's Store. The owners lived in the back of the store in a small apartment. Inside the shelves were stocked with canned goods and produce. Cookies and candy were displayed out on the counter in glass jars to tempt the most frugal shoppers. Produce was displayed in the baskets and crates around the store. Smith's Store was the only place in town with telephone service, so if a call came to the store, Mr. Smith wrote the message and carried it to the intended destination. Most families could not afford telephone service, so they were very grateful to Mr. Smith for this community act. The store had a bench outside where the area men loved to gather. One man who loved to sit on Smith's bench was L. L. Kinney. His wife was a school teacher and he was a professor from Illinois.

Smith Store Produce

When he came to Florida, he worked for a while for Mr. Paul until he suffered blindness from being hit with a baseball. Mr. Billy Wheeler remembers guiding him to the seat where his friends met and drank and talked about everything under the sun. Shirley (Craig) Markham tells that Mr. Kinney enjoyed sharing his love for the arts and poetry with the girls who walked him around Watertown, but they were never asked to take him to the bench, for that was just for the men folk.

Smith's Sinclair Station

Shirley Craig's father, Robert, was a Methodist boy from Bolivar, Missouri, but her mother, Josephine, was a Catholic girl from New York. She was the postmistress of the post office in Watertown. The little wooden building had a small window that opened out onto a front porch where residents picked up their mail. It was a far cry from her roots but for Watertown, she worked in the hub of business.

Josephine was, at heart, a city girl. The Paul family brought their lavish lifestyle with them when they came from Wisconsin. They took long trips to California on the Watertown train car set up as a party car and had a vacation home on Atlantic Beach. While Mrs. Paul was in Watertown, she enjoyed the Hollingsworth House, opening the luxurious ballroom to guests on occasion.

Josephine Craig was thrilled to receive her invitation but she knew she had no suitable clothes for such an affair. Mrs. Paul understood and loaned her an exquisite gown for the evening. However, she was not escorted by her husband. She brought Shirley with her. Robert had no desire for the sophistication of city folks. Although she was only four years old, Shirley remembered her mother was beautiful that night, but the child was unhappy to see the unfamiliar side of her mother. Robert was a loving husband and father and they had many good years together, perhaps intrigued by their differences.

The Hollingsworth House was a beautiful home that stood out in Watertown. The people of Watertown described it like a mansion. There was a black man who served as the butler. What a striking contrast this was to the 1920's Watertown! He was dressed in a white uniform with a black tie and he formally greeted the guests, announcing their arrival at the door.

There was even a swimming pool and the children were allowed to swim there for twenty-five cents. There wasn't a lot of entertainment for the children in Watertown, so they were happy to use the pool. Later on, the Hollingsworth House was the USO location for the military who were stationed in the area.

The families of the company town were hard working people. Many of them were holiness people, but when their security was lost in the Great Depression, they were just as affected as their neighbors. What would happen to them now? How could they manage if they had no jobs? How would they feed their families? Only those who trusted in God were comforted, and knew He was watching over His children, and like the sparrow and the lilies of the field, He would provide for their needs… and beautifully.

Did they have the faith they needed to get through these lean years? How could they look Mr. Bill Phillips in the eye when he came to collect the rent for A.E. Paul? No one had money for a lot of fine luxuries, but an employee at the saw mill felt satisfied to be able to provide for his family.

The Watertown Bank was doing so well at first, it was the fifth largest bank in Columbia County. In 1919, they recorded funds at $35,978.87. The citizens were all getting ahead financially. In fact, some were traveling by train to the beaches for a day in the sun. The May 30th, 1919 Citizen Reporter advertised Seaboard Air Line Railway low Sunday rates to Pablo and Atlantic Beach as an opportunity to visit Jacksonville or the beaches on Sunday. The fare from Watertown to Atlantic Beach was $1.95, and for $1.80, one could go to Pablo Beach.

In 1929, the Great Depression hit the entire country and the Watertown Bank fell victim to the economic crisis. The bank caught fire soon after and the residents tell how the bank vault sat outside the charred remains of the building for weeks.

Then came the mid-1930's. Charles "Buddy" Wiggins was just nine years old and remembers the good

Watertown Logging Train

times he shared with his dad at Watertown's logging camp. He said sections of track(spurs) were laid out in different directions as temporary camps were relocated and scattered as needed. Houses were simply lifted and placed on railroad cars to be taken to the next site.

Skidders were used to back empty log cars to the area of fallen trees. Mules were used to pull the cables out into the brush. The cables had claws that hooked into the logs, then took the logs by train back to the lumber mill to be dumped into Alligator Lake. The logs were all kept in the lake so they were easier to cut. Then they were loaded onto the train cars. The old steam locomotives equipped with smoke arresters on the smokestack hauled the logs to the mill. Men of all ages liked to run the switch engine, nicknamed the "Eight Spot." The Watertown Northern Railroad was called the Moonshine Line (built around 1880), because of the turpentine stills in the woods, but 'other stills' were found as the Paul's operations grew.

One of the old spur tracks ended near the mill in front of the Wiggins house. The load of logs were heavy as they were pulled down the tracks by that big train; smoke was belching from the stack. Soon the loads were not quite as heavy as the work had dwindled from the effects of the Depression. Two weeks had passed without a load. Then three weeks passed and still no load was in sight. The men from the mill were losing confidence, and feared the mill would be shut down. Prayers were going out asking God to send them work. They were at the end of

Nelson Brady with wife Agnes and Alice 'Dinky' Brady

their rope! Then one summer night, about midnight, Buddy Wiggins heard the distant blasting of a train's whistle. He jumped up and ran like lightning to his father's room, shouting, "Dad! Dad! The train is coming! The log train is coming!"

In a split second, the man was dressed and headed for the door, saying, "Come on, Son, let's go meet that train!" They walked for a few minutes and they could hear the train as it moved slowly on the tracks. Out of the shadows, around a curve there came a beautiful sight ...hope for his family. Then Mr. Henry, the engineer, slowly brought the train to a stop and waved for the two to come aboard. The steam was hissing. Then he sounded two blows of the old whistle and the black train rumbled to life, as it chugged down the

Alton Hall with Mildred Brady Hall and baby Gerry Hall

tracks to the mill yard. And suddenly, it was a magnificent night!

God had just answered prayer. This new supply of logs assured their jobs for at least the next month. Again their needs were supplied 'according to His riches in glory!'

CHAPTER XVII

All Shapes, Sizes, Ages, Too: Jesus Has A Plan For You

Families were poor but blessed in every way that mattered, when they brought home the spiritual food that nourished the covenant keepers. Hard times have been known to bring the hard sinner man to his knees, and his prayers get answered!

("Be not forgetful to entertain strangers: for thereby some have entertained angels unawares. Hebrews 13:2 KJV). Even the hoboes who camped around Alligator Lake in Watertown all knew this was a blessed area. Beyond the tracks, the lake was surrounded by underbrush and forest, except for a small clearing that was known as "Hobo Town."

Freight cars passed through Watertown on the route between New Orleans and Jacksonville and slowed down at the crossing. Several men, down on their luck, would jump aboard, riding inside, on top or even in the gondola in search of a meal or a place to spend the night.

Some of the hoboes were drifters with no goals in life. Others were educated but out of work. They all had stories to tell. Some of their stories were of a community called Watertown, where the people were very poor, but none so poor they couldn't share their provisions with a hungry traveler. Secret codes and chits were made on posts and trees, passed on so the next arrivals to Hobo Town knew where to go for a meal. It is amazing how God was using even the lowly hobo in His remarkable plan for His people. By their sacrificing for a stranger, they were blessed: ("Give, and it shall be given unto you; good measure, pressed down, and shaken together, and running over, shall men give into your bosom. For with the same measure that ye mete withal, it shall be measured to you again." Luke 6:38 KJV). This is not just a good thought, it is the PROMISE from GOD! It works!

We must take care of our neighbors, looking out for one another.

In the early years of Watertown, a midwife cared for families when no doctor was available. Miss Minnie, a petite black woman, had been a memorable part of the history of the company town.

Elsie Cortez carried her big black satchel, selling her salves and ointments door to door. The children watched her a little suspiciously as she trudged through the streets in her long dark skirt. Her Hispanic/Indian heritage was evident in her high cheek bones and dark skin; spicy foods she consumed emitted a pungent scent as she passed by.

Watertown Crossing had a store called Gainus Grocery, owned by a black man and patronized by the neighborhood black families. Occasionally, the young men from one of the white families would feel a little adventurous and sneak over to the Crossing area to play the slot machines in the Gainus Grocery.

Others were lured to the High Hat Club, a night club owned by Mabel Howard, a black woman from south Florida. Rumors said she had once worked in Miami for a man called 'Al Capone.' Whether this was true or not, the rumor attracted the curious young people who were drawn to the night life and the music.

The holiness families knew they needed the hand of God to steady the morals in the home. Tent revivals were being set up in the area and souls were being saved.

The Great Depression had made its impact on Watertown and the country but the revivals were also springing up around the area. Evangelist C. B. Daniels and gospel songwriter and evangelist, Charlie Tillman, held revivals in the area of Watertown. The generations of today are still reaping the benefits of renewed covenants made at those camp meetings! When people meet with God, lives

The 1954 Watertown School yearbook is filled with old memories of Christmas past.

are changed for the better.

Christian values were beginning to be formed and treasured. Even the schools were having Christmas plays and parties to celebrate the birth of Jesus. Mrs. Charlotte Horton Young has graciously shared her precious childhood memories and I feel as though I was there, waiting for Santa and excitedly talking about the school play!

Mrs. Annie B. Mershon's
1st & 2nd grade classes

Whether the memories are of the time Santa Claus came to their school or when the Christmas story was performed and the wise men and shepherds all wore bed sheet robes, these are the memories that fill the hearts of our aging grandparents today.

Mrs. Lois Revel's
3rd & 4th grade classes

Wherever you spent your childhood, there are great times to look back on, loved ones who have made an impact on your life. For the holiness family, most of the wonderful times are events and conversations that convey God's grace and love, but the past is a garden, where we harvest crops of strength and the fortitude for tough times ahead; a time for spiritual growth, as we each search for our Holy Ground.

These are memories all our own. The people are forever cherished. Thank You, Lord, for precious memories! They will always be treasured!

I have visited the past, Lord, and I see the pains and fears that

Mr. Paul Giebeig's
5th & 6th grade classes

brought this land to its knees. I have met many saints of God and watched as their families have cried out to You! I have seen industry come and go and I have seen dreams wither and die. I have read countless census and I feel as though these people are my families.

I can hear the brogue of Patrick O'Neal and listen for the children giggling as they call out for 'Uncle Pat!' What a wise man he was, too! Educated in New York, he moved to Florida where he met and fell in love with Eva Murray, (Mamie Murray Westberry's sister). At the wedding, W.H. Westberry stood up for his Irish friend who was to become his brother-in-law.

Patrick and Eva had four children: Johnny O'Neal, Mary, Suzie and Nellie. I hear Johnny was a handsome man. He left at least one lady back home remembering her crush on him. Mary O'Neal married a man named Wheeler and had one child; with her second husband, (Ellis), she had four children. Suzie was married to H.W. Eubanks, (son of Noah Wright Eubanks and Lucy Eubanks), and had nine children. They are: Ramona (Carpenter), Willerdine (never married), Christine (Moody), Eddie Alex (returned to heaven as an infant), Linda Jean (Paul, no relation to A.E. Paul), Patrick Wayne, Ivonne (Blake), Michael Dale and Bobby Wright O'Neal. Nellie was the last of the children.

I have found the endless rows of faces of dear saints of God; cried when I heard that Eddie Alex Eubanks died as an infant and mourned with Suzie as she buried her tiny son. I was joyous when I met Ramona Eubanks who married a Carpenter boy. I have learned to imagine a face attached to names like: Bud Brady and his sister, Alice 'Dinky' Brady Parker, Tommie (Stuart) Benton, Thomas Trammel from the Commissary, the barber who lived near Highway 90, named Ellzey.

I heard about Mildred Hall who worked at Lake Shore Hospital in the kitchen, the Jarrett sisters who ran the dairy where you could get the best milk and also the freshest eggs. Belle Jarett was a teacher and her sister, Leona Prestwood had a son named Jack who joined the Air Force during the war.

I learned the Smith family, who owned the grocery store in Watertown, bought a nice brick home when the Smiths retired. I wish I could have been there to give them a house warming gift. They deserved a nice home after living in the back of the store for all those years!

I was told that Patrick O'Neal picked up the mail bag that hung by the railroad station at its drop and then carried it to Josephine Craig at the post office. Patrick was a tall man so it wasn't so hard to visualize him reaching for the mail bag. I do believe Josephine, (daughter of Sim Kirby), who was the post mistress and mother of Shirley Craig, and wife of Robert, looked forward to seeing the tall mail carrier. After all, he was educated in New York and she came from the same state; probably they discussed all the people and places they left behind, and if Mr. L. L. Kinney came in, the three could talk about the fine arts, and maybe wonder if their Watertown would ever have an arts center or opera house.

A map of Watertown was drawn for me and I saw where Sim Kirby, Mattie Lee Davis, the Brady family and Ethel Skinner lived. Beatrice Williams and Woodrow Bryant lived on the same road and I even was told about Humpy, the cow (with the bell around her neck) who was kept in the field next to the cornfield. I could see the face Bud Brady made when his mom grabbed him by the ear to make him go to church and act like a gentleman. Of course, the Bradys were faithful to the Congregational Holiness Church so Bud knew any horseplay would have to be done when the Lord's Word wasn't being preached. Then a bunch of the young men would meet in the church yard for a game of tackle football.

All these families are like the ones we know today, Lord, even some of the names are the same, just a different generation. Life runs in cycles and nothing really changes. I can see even then there were wars and rumors of wars.

The people all brought their fried chicken to 'dinners on the grounds,' and there was probably even a Sister Dorothy Harden who made the best 'nanner puddin' in the whole south. She may have been a Margaret or Bess but I'm sure some saintly sister had a special offering to the church dinners, just like our precious Sister 'Dot.' A few of those women could 'cut a rug' or had a 'hallelujah heydey' when "It's A Grand And Glorious Feeling," was sung, (just like Sister 'Dot' Harden).

In old Watertown, life continued with families, careers, finances, crisis, and eventually a funeral. What can be learned from this life cycle never to be broken! ("But as the days of Noah were, so shall also the coming of the Son of man be. For as in the days that were before the flood they were eating and drinking, marrying and giving in marriage, until the day that Noah entered into the ark, and knew not until the flood came, and took them all away; so shall also the coming of the Son of man be. Then shall two be in the field; the one shall be taken, and the other left. Two women shall be grinding at the mill; the one shall be taken, and the other left. Watch therefore: for ye know not what hour your Lord doth come." Matthew 24:37-42 KJV).

You have shown me how easily misled we are. These people were all good people I could have considered my friends for life. Yet even on this journey, I was getting caught up in the day-to-day lives and routines of the ones You have sent me to study. It never occurred to me I might have seen some clue to alert me to the dangers and pitfalls of allowing routines of every day life to dull our senses, making us insensitive to Your voice, or to be ready for the sounding trumpet. What a treasured lesson learned at this stop in my journey to find Holy Ground! I will always cherish the memories of the ancestors I have met in Old Watertown!

The ancestors I visited were patriots, but above that, they were Christians. The wars came and the young men rallied without hesitation. This was, as one grandmother said, "their God-given duty to serve their country and keep our families free." As the old buses rolled out of town, soldiers waved proudly, mothers and wives tearfully said good-bye, the fathers held back their emotions. These men would have joined their sons in a flash, if their government would allow it. (That was the emotion of regret). The older men saw their grown sons, actually young men, going to war, and their hearts broke as they pleaded with God, ' Please don't let my son have to see all the horrors I had to face in my war days.' (That emotion was pure sorrow). Then they ran along the side of the bus, hoping to get one more glimpse of that soldier son, and they smiled broadly as they wiped away a tear. (That emotion was pride) That is why America has nothing to fear. God (and the family of God, led by Him) has everything under control. We are protected by God's covenant. ("What shall we then say to these things? If God be for us, who can be against us?" Romans 8:31 KJV).

*On July 30, 1956, our nation adopted the motto: 'In God

- 85 -

We Trust.' This motto originated during the Civil War when the Secretary of the Treasury, Salmon P. Chase, was asked by Rev. M.R. Watkinson, of Ridleyville, Pennsylvania, to recognize 'the Almighty God in some form in our coins.' Chase requested Congress to pass a law changing the 2-cent piece to include the inscription "In God We Trust." The law was passed on April 22, 1864 and that year the 2-cent coin was the first to bear the motto. Eventually, all coins and currency adopted the inscription. (*Used by permission).

The platform of the First Full Gospel Church has a station for two flags, one for the American flag and the other for the Christian flag. We all proudly salute the American flag, as we quote, 'ONE NATION ~ UNDER GOD! One corridor wall displays our church family's soldiers. On another wall in the corridor are pictures of men and women of God who have gone to receive their crowns and robes. ("His lord said unto him, "Well done, good and faithful servant; thou hast been faithful over a few things, I will make thee ruler over many things: enter thou into the joy of thy lord." Matthew 25:23 KJV).

Did they find Holy Ground, a haven of rest, before passing on to their rewards? Did any of these dear old saints embark on such a journey as You have mapped for me? You have sent me exploring through the generations to teach me wisdom and knowledge. You want me to enter into Your perfect peace where time and matter is insignificant when placed before the magnificence of Your glory. I lifted my hands to praise Him, the altar was before me and the Bible was open on the showbread table. I stopped and touched the Holy Word as I read Genesis Chapter 35, starting with verse one. And it was as though an angel was standing before me, ministering to my heart, mind and soul.

I remembered this story of Jacob when I taught the teen Sunday School Class. Jacob had just deceived Isaac and had taken away the birthright blessing that rightfully was to be given to Esau. Now he was running for his very life. Jacob had gone to Bethel and had a vision, a ladder on which angels ascended and descended. The Book of Genesis, chapter 28, verse 13-14 KJV : "And behold, the Lord stood above it, and said, I am the Lord God of Abraham thy father, and the God of Isaac: the land whereon thou liest, to thee will I give it, and to thy seed; And thy seed shall be as the dust of the earth, and thou shalt spread abroad to the west, and to the east, and to the north, and to the south: and in thee and in thy seed shall all the families of the earth be blessed." But then, the pages of His Holy Word had drawn me to Genesis 35:11-15. God told Jacob to go BACK to where he first met God who appeared before him when he had fled from Esau, BACK to BETHEL! The message was for Jacob to put away all his foreign gods (any distraction) that took the place of God in their lives, purify themselves (sanctify themselves) and return to Bethel (the altar) to seek the God that keeps you from the day of distress and will never leave you. God said to Jacob, there will be enemy attacks, but none would pursue Jacob and his sons (the anointed, sanctified children of God) and when Jacob came back to the altar, he received a new name, (written down in Glory), Israel.

Now it was all becoming very clear to me! My search began as a little girl who wandered in aimlessness, protected by God as He led me to a powerful anointing! Then He took me back to not only meet the saints who struggled for the religious freedoms we take for granted, and the pampered Christians we've become, but to see that just as Jesus Christ is the same, yesterday and today and forever, so is man. Mankind is forever struggling with the lust of the flesh, the desires of the human race, but knowing a stronger force, a God whose power dominates the battles we face. In weakness, we turn from God so we must strive to strengthen the Spirit man within us, that we may be spared on that great judgment day! That's why He brought me back to the present day Christians. We all need to do our part to win the lost and to see God's amazing miracles make the world sit up and take notice!

I looked at the big Bible and said, "Lord, we already have a Bible full of Your Word and Your promises for mankind. How can we get Your Word out to the world? The Bible has been around for a long time and it has stood the test of nations at war! The world is so cynical now and distrusting. I know how they feel but I don't know how to give them what they need to find You and their own Holy Ground!"

And God said, "Tell my children to send out the Word that God loves them and wants to be their Father, to protect and to provide for them. They need to build their faith on the promises I have already fulfilled, and the belief that I will never stop. I make my covenant to last from the beginning of time to the end of the world. For now, I am waiting for them to come unto Me, that they may find rest from the weary land. I am waiting …but not for long! For soon the Eastern skies will break and Jesus the Christ will appear to bring my children home, and the time is very near!"

I turned around and my memory took me back to the night I had a vision. I was sitting in my usual seat and as I glanced towards the altar I saw what appeared to be a new dimension in time. I saw C.A. Boston running for heaven's gates, with the exuberance of a young man who had made his first homerun! For indeed he was running Home!

Chapter XVIII

You Won't Have A Testimony Until You've Been Tested

One Sunday, I asked for testimonies for a book I was writing, because I wanted the lost to hear our victories through Christ Jesus. May God be praised and you blessed!

1. C.A. AND BETTY BOSTON AND FAMILY

C.A. Boston was baptized in the First Full Gospel Church by Pastor Thomas Brown and Dave Kirkman, [Pentecostal preachers] In attendance was Stanley D. Ellis, a young preacher. Brother C.A. Boston (Clarence Alva Boston) attended the First Full Gospel Church for 25 years. He was born on the 4th of July, 1931, a son of Alva and Vera Boston. His father was a well-loved preacher at the church when it

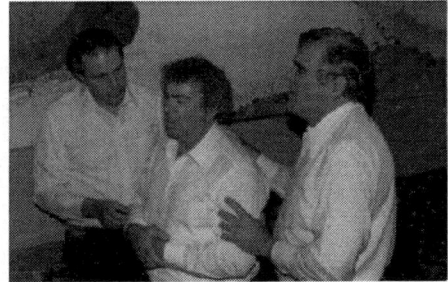

Dave Kirkman, C.A. & Thomas Brown

was called the Congregational Holiness. C.A. had many friends throughout his life. If someone had a need that was to be handled by the church funds, he was apt to just reach into his pocket instead and give it to you, no questions asked. He had B&B's Seafood Market for nearly 25 years, but his greatest pride and passion, next to God, was the love he had for his four daughters and his wife of 56 years, Betty Poitevint.

Brother C.A. and Sister Betty were all smiles on November 24, 2006, as they posed for pictures

C.A. Boston, with his four daughters, grandchildren, and great grandchildren!

at their daughter Terri's wedding to Danny Brown, son of James and Joyce Brown, the preacher who baptized Terri's father, C.A. Boston).

Family Group (L-R):
Patricia Stuart, Rhonda Russell, Terri Brown, C.A., Rita Swisher, and wife, Betty

Even during his last days, C.A. always had a smile on his face and his testimony, "I want to thank God for everything he's done for me and my family…" It is with sorrow I tell you Clarence Alva Boston died on January 31st, 2008, but the angels rejoice at his homegoing and we will meet again in heavenly places!

It seems this story is just about C.A. but this is not so. One quiet and humble lady would be satisfied enough to know her husband was being honored. Betty Boston is what makes this family so strong in the Lord. With her genteel voice, she raised her daughters with poise and charm. She has a grace about her that bespeaks the love of God. ("Who can find a virtuous woman? For her price is far above rubies." Proverbs 31:10 KJV). Sister Betty Boston is that woman, for she is a source of compassion and love to all who are blessed enough to meet her.

Danny and Terri (Boston) Brown, C.A. and Betty Boston

2. GEORGE BOSTON

One cannot say the name Brother George Boston of the First Full Gospel Church without smiling. He is a brother of C.A. Boston, but he is a force to be reckoned with all on his own.

George Boston is a big man in his mid-70's but he has a fervor for the mission field that overcomes the odds. Many times he has started out for underprivileged countries in a bus or truck that is held together more by a prayer than nuts and bolts, and Bibles were delivered! Even when he became ill, he refused to be kept down.

"The old devil thinks he's got me this time, but he ain't, 'cause me and God, we're in this thing together and my God ain't ready to quit and neither am I." And with a big, friendly smile he grips your hand in a firm handshake and says, "Pray for me; we're going back!"

Each time he returns with a report, we hear of the churches he has built or the lost souls that were saved, being sure no one gives credit

Adam and George Boston

to anyone but Jesus Christ for all the success stories. Sometimes he tells how they overcame impossible situations with the help of the Almighty God he serves. And for just a moment, you almost forget that he's talking about God, instead of an old friend who goes with him, straps on a tool belt and gets the job done. He rarely leaves a service that he doesn't invite others to join him on a trip and see the miracles of God. [George Boston]

3. BETTY (BROWN) BAKER

Testimony stories build faith. One of my favorite stories, Lord, is the one Betty Baker had to tell. Her mother was the same Mary Ensley Brown, (sister of Mattie Lee Davis) who lived in Old Watertown. Brother Alva Boston baptized 'Granny' Ensley Brown in the 1960's in Deep Creek and Brother John Dortch baptized Sister Betty in Watertown Lake in 1947. Betty says her memory takes her back to those old baptism songs, 'Shall We Gather At the River?' and the saints

Mary Ensley Brown

started shouting in the water as the blessings flowed! Betty and Mary (Brown) Meads sang with their brother James and his wife Joyce to form the Brown quartet. The harmony was beautiful and the Spirit was pleased! Sister Eubanks shouted in the Spirit until her hair came down! Granny Brown's heart was full as she heard her children singing praises to God! Brother Dortch loved the old song, 'I Can Almost See the Light.' "I can remember sitting by that red-hot pot belly stove in the middle of the church. There were a lot of 'Dinners on the Grounds' and music all the time. Brother Boston used to grab his ear and shout as he was preaching and Brother Dortch's favorite saying was, "sang that song!" Then when Brother Ulis Taylor became the preacher, he said, 'You just can't beat those Brown quartet girls!' Then he picked up his guitar and offered a special song of praise to the Lord. Those memories make me strong as I see pictures and people who blessed me.

Below, are some of Sister Betty's favorite pictures:

William, Betty, Thomas and James
Her sisters were Mary (Meads) and Nellie Ruth

Betty Baker, Linda Davis, and
Felix Baker (Betty's husband).

Gene and Betty (Brown) Powell had two children, Harold Powell, born on September 1st, 1956 and Linda (Powell) Davis, born on June 10th, 1958. Years later, Betty met and married Felix Baker who now attends church faithfully with his wife. Betty attributes her strong faith to her mama. "She always had us in church, no matter what the occasion was, and I'm thankful. This, I believe is why I came back to God. She raised us up to love the Lord and to know He was watching out for us. I may have drifted away for a while but I'm back where I belong and this is where I am going to stay. I would like to be just like my mama. My children were raised in the church the way she did with us."

Her mother's prayers were mighty! She lived her beliefs. Her legacy will forever remain a part of God's covenant. She loved God and God honored her forever.

4. JAMES AND JOYCE BROWN

Lord, You have given me so many windows to gaze into, to see Your love in action with Your children. I treasure the insight You have given to me! The blessings Your children have received and shared with others is Your covenant with them! You are the reason for their bountiful lives!

I would like to share a story of a godly man. James H. Brown was born on the 19th of September in 1935, in Elmore County, Ala., where he left in 1947, at the age of 12, to move to Lake City. His mother, Mary Ensley Brown, was a devout Christian woman. His father was led to salvation later in life by a man named Reverend Dicks. James was saved in 1960, at the age of 24 in the morning service and that night his wife, Joyce, got saved.

Lake City Reporter & Columbia Gazette
PAGE 22   Lake City, Fla., Thursday, March 16, 1967

New Church Started

Shown breaking ground for the new Congregational Holiness Church of Watertown are Deacon James Brown and the Rev. Ulis Taylor, pastor, who started the building fund. Ground for the new church was broken last week. The new building will be designed to seat approximately 300 people. (Photo by Paul Roy).

They worked for the Lord for many years; she played the piano, and he was a deacon, Sunday School superintendent, minister and even did janitorial work as was needed. Wherever God needed a servant, James was willing to be that man. With Joyce by his side, he was a true worker for God. Raised by his holiness mother, he learned honesty and integrity at an early age.

I asked Brother James, "If you could give your best advice to someone today, what would you say?" He said, "Turn your life over to God quickly, today ~ immediately! If you are married, this will keep you married… happily married. If you are not married, don't give a second glance to someone who is not a Christian. You won't change them, but they will drag you down into sin. And if you're wanting to get married and not a good Christian yourself, start back at where I said, 'Turn your life over to God.'"

"My wife and I have been married for 55 years. We have never been separated. God has blessed us with two wonderful children, although they are both grown now.

James D. 'Danny' Brown was born June 14th, 1958, and Deborah Y. Brown (Raines) was born on March 11, 1960. They were active in Sunday School while they were growing up."

As the Browns get older, their children with homes of their own, they miss the

The Browns with chihahua 'Buddy'

joy that comes from having a little one to love and about whom to share memories. God sent them a little friend and companion, named Buddy, that completes their happy home. Buddy can always make the Browns smile!

Danny married Terri Boston, daughter of C.A. Boston on November 24th, 2006, at a wedding held at First Full Gospel Church. (See inset on the Boston page). God has richly blessed the Brown family; they showed love in action!

5. MARSHALL AND LINDA DAVIS

These two wonderful saints of God are examples of what a Christian should be! They came to us in our times of crisis and walked us right through it. Jesus Christ lives in their hearts. He has such a mighty presence within them that you can't look at them without seeing God! I will never forget the day I heard Linda coming down the corridor in the hospital! I had just been told I was being released but I would have to be sent to a convalescent care center. Tears filled my eyes and I felt my heart breaking. I just wanted to go home but I had no one to manage my home nursing care. Then I sat up in bed as I heard Linda coming, calling out as she was approaching my room, "Hold on, Sister, I'm comin!" And she was all I needed. She took over, told the nurses and doctors exactly what was on her mind and home we

Linda and Marshall Davis

went, with Linda and Marshall leading the way! There is nothing I can say or do that would be equal repayment for everything they have done for us!

Marshall is a big man with a bigger heart. One only has to speak the name, Jesus, to see the tears roll down his cheeks. Unashamed of his tears, he tells you how much he loves his Saviour. He is asked to sing nearly every week at church, not because he has a trained voice, but because when he sings his heart touches the Throne of God. Standing humbly in farmer overalls, Marshall sings under a heavy anointing, because he's singing for Jesus. And nobody does it better than the man named Marshall, for he has felt the nail-scarred hands of Jesus and walked with Him to Calvary. He knows first-hand about precious salvation and the price that had to be paid for it. This is Marshall's testimony:

"I think God has always been a big part of my life. I got started in church because my wife was raised in the church. (Her mother is Betty Brown Baker). The Browns have always been strong Christians but when I met Linda, I drew her away from church for a while. But I thank God she went back because soon, I was ready to join her there."

"I was a truck driver and sometimes I was on the road quite a bit. All of a sudden, it seemed like all I could do was cry! This was on a Sunday and I was driving that rig down the highway, crying my eyes out. I knew then I was under conviction of God. I cried all day! I couldn't wait to get back home to the family. I knew they would help me to pray the sinner's prayer and I gave my life over to the Lord."

"There is no way to write down what God has done for me, how He has blessed me in my life since I have known Him in this special way. I just thank Him every day… I just praise Him every day and I pray I am not a disappointment to Him."

"My advice is to try every second of your life to obey Him and His way. Walk in His Light and keep lifting up the name of Jesus! I talk to God like I do anyone else and I know He loves me and I love Him! He just wants you to come and talk with Him… today!"

Linda and Marshall were married on March 19th, 1994 and God truly joined this couple in Holy Matrimony. He had a plan for them. They are two of the greatest church workers anyone could ever find. Linda tells about some of her experiences in her own testimony: "I would like to thank the Lord for Granny Ensley Brown. She is why I'm in church today. God has answered many prayers in my life because my Granny taught me to keep on praying and have faith no matter what we are going through. We serve a great big God! The Lord uses people to make us strong and Helen Hill is a good example. When she had cancer, I was her caregiver throughout her surgery and recovery, and through that experience, my faith grew strong! The Lord helped me so I could be there for her. She is an amazing woman and I thank God, He sent her my way!"

"I also thank God for a Christian home. Being raised by generations of Christians, I also wanted my children to be brought up in a Christian home. My daughter, Tonya was born on January 8th, 1979 and my son, Randy was born on December 7th, 1981. They were both actively involved in Sunday School, Bible studies and youth groups. Both of my children were baptized in 1989 and Randy married Amber in 2002 in a ceremony held at First Full Gospel Church. These are wonderful memories but I have earlier memories that were very special, too."

"My mama, Betty Baker, used to sing and play the piano. Her voice was beautiful! I remember watching her sitting at the piano with long, black hair. Granny Brown was so faithful to God and I can remember listening to all the powerful prayers and testimonies! The wooden benches used to crack and pop. Mama used to put us down on the floor so we could sleep while they had church. People all around us were shouting but we never got stepped on! The church people were our family. We had dinners on the grounds held under shelters and the young people would play volleyball and softball. At Easter, we had Easter egg hunts. Sometimes the pastor, (Uncle Thomas Brown, for one), would hide the eggs. There are four ministers that I remember as my pastor, Thomas Brown, Ulis Taylor, Forest Combs, and Stan Ellis. When I was 11 or 12, it was my job to carry a glass of water to Brother Ulis Taylor. It felt like an important job to me."

"Sister Betty Combs, wife of Forest Combs, had Bible study on Wednesday nights. When my children were 8 or 9, they loved to hunt Bible verses in the class. My son, Randy, usually beat out even the adults as they all tried to race to find the scripture. Watching them filled me with pride! I'm still proud of both of my children. I'm waiting to see my prayers answered when I see them sitting in church together again, with mama. Lord, keep my children safe and make sure nothing keeps them from your salvation!" [Linda Davis]

Tonya, Randy, and Mom

The photo on the right is a few of the usual kitchen crew, cooking for a dinner honoring C.A. Boston for years of Christian service to our church. This group specializes in roll up your sleeves technology, and you bless us all!

Robbie Geiger, Janice & Jimmy Davis, Heyward Christie, Linda & Marshall Davis

6. JIMMY AND JANICE DAVIS AND FAMILY

The only thing I have NOT seen this family pour their hearts and energy into is the job of preaching the Gospel, but then they don't have to; their lives speak the gospel. This is the testimony of Janice Davis: "I want to thank the Lord first for saving me at an early age. My parents Jake and Betty Raulerson weren't saved but every Sunday, they sent all their kids to church. We attended Pine Grove Baptist Church and by the time I was eleven my parents got saved and then they were not only sending us, but they were going with us! When I got married to Jimmy Davis in 1981, I started going to the Lake City, (Florida), Church of God. We started our family, (Vicky, Heather, and Crystal) and took them to church with us.

Jimmy & Janice Davis

When Heather turned four, she started singing in church. Her first song was "Dear Mr. Jesus," and she touched many hearts."

"My parents were attending the First Full Gospel Church and when Sunday night came, they asked if we would let them take

Heather with them so she could sing for the church service. We were proud to know she was singing for Jesus. One night we decided to go listen to her sing. and we felt the powerful Spirit in the church. Jimmy and I started praying the Lord would lead us to the church where He wanted us to be.Two weeks later we started coming to the First Full Gospel Church. About a month later, we became the youth leaders in the church, a position we held for about two years. When my dad, Jake got ill, we couldn't give 100% to the youth so we decided to give it up. We still helped out wherever we were needed but we claim no credit for ourselves. It's all God! We could never do anything without Him. I praise God for my healing and my family. I am expecting God to save the rest of my family before He calls me home or comes back in the Rapture."
[Janice Raulerson Davis]

Top photo #1: (Back L-R) Crystal, Jimmy, Vicky, Janice, & Heather. Top photo #2: Jimmy & Janice Davis. Top photo #3: Robbie & Heather (Davis) Geiger. Middle photo #1: Hunter Bryson. #2: Crystal (Davis) Bryson. #3: Matt Bryson. Bottom photo #1: Ben Davis. #2: Emma Leigh Green. #3: Danny Green and Vicky (Davis) Green.

On the right are favorite pictures of the Davis family: Jimmy and his three daughters all teach Sunday School. Janice volunteers everywhere!

7. FRANCIS DAVIS, MOTHER OF JIMMY DAVIS

After writing the testimony and including the pictures of the Raulerson-Davis family, I would be amiss if I didn't include this beautiful lady. Her husband was Ben Davis, whose photograph graces the wall of saints in the corridor of the church. Sister Francis is 'Granny.' to everybody. She enters the church services with a smile on her face and praise on her lips. She never has an unkind word for anyone. I asked Sister Davis to say a few words about the Lord. She said, "Being a Christian means everything to me. I love Jesus with all my heart, soul and mind! He's my everything ~ my food when I am hungry, water for my thirst, and my companion when I'm lonely. But I love Jesus most of all, because He saved my soul and He keeps me every day. He is my

Francis Davis

soon Coming King! If you don't know Jesus, let Him save you today and you"ll never be sorry!" [Francis Davis]

8. GREG DAVIS

Francis' son Greg is a familiar face at the First Full Gospel; not just on Sunday. He is one of our most enthusiastic supporter of the Monday Prayer Group. He stands on his Solid Rock and urges everyone to do the same! He always has a smile for his joy is from God!

Greg Davis

9. HEYWARD AND DEBORAH CHRISTIE

If there's a celebration, you're likely to see Heyward Christie in the church kitchen. He will be the friendly, smiling man in the apron serving up all the barbecued meats. He has such a gentle spirit it is

Deborah & 'Santa' Heyward Christie

no wonder he was chosen to fill the vacancy in the deacon position when C.A. Boston retired. He was also chosen several times to play the jolly role of Santa Claus. Mrs. Deborah 'Santa' Christie says 'Santa' is good to her year 'round. 'Mrs. [Deborah] 'Claus' Christie is a caring, praying woman who loves God first. She is

Heyward & Deborah Christie

a blessing to us all. The Christies have been married since the 20th of October, 1975 and have one son, Michael born November 25th, 1980. Do they have a blessed marriage? Yes, but blessings are earned. Every marriage takes work. Heyward says their marriage works because they respect each other and keep the Spirit of God in their lives daily.. ("But the fruit of the Spirit is love, joy, peace, longsuffering, gentleness, goodness, faith, meekness, temperance: against such there is no Law." Gal. 5:22,23 KJV).

10. AARON AND LISA BUTLER AND FAMILY

The Butler family has been a very welcomed group in First Full Gospel. Their family has a strong spiritual foundation that overflows throughout the service. They encourage our youth to grow with the Lord and any altar service will find the Butler family helping someone pray through. Sister Lisa has a sweet spirit and helps everyone. Brother Aaron is usually just standing back with a sheepish grin but he has his hand on the pulse of any situation. Shelby sings with the voice of an angel but anyone who knows her sees her spiritual strength. She has been walking with God for a very long time;

The Butler Family

she's a real prayer warrior! Jarrod Butler is becoming a talented musician as well. He loves a good time and a good joke. He reminds me of Samson, not for physical strength, but for his boyish joy and exuberance. One day we will hear about all the great things he has done for the Lord, but it would do him well to thank God each day for two parents who love him enough to guide him into heavenly places. Lisa Butler wrote out her testimony in hopes it would serve others as they seek a closer walk with God.

"My testimony is how God used our children to draw us closer to Him and each other. My husband and I were high school sweethearts. We graduated from Columbia High School in Lake City, Florida, in 1986. Not long after graduating, Aaron decided to join the Marines. On December 18th, 1987, before he left for Basic Training, Aaron asked me to marry him and of course, I said yes. Our wedding date was December 17th, 1988. Approximately 2 years later Aaron was working full time in Law Enforcement and an Active Reservist in the United States Marine Corps when we found out I was pregnant with our first child. We had not been trying to get pregnant; 'it just happened,' we thought. One day we were having a serious disagreement and our emotions were riding high. We both said hurtful things to each other and as the day progressed, we were actually avoiding each other. This was the first of many lessons God would teach us. Around 4:00 pm that same afternoon, the phone rang and Aaron was told his reserve unit had been activated and they would be leaving for Iraq in the next few weeks. After that phone conversation, we were both scared and felt terrible for hurting each other, knowing that the next several days or months could change our lives forever."

"The next few weeks were consumed with us preparing everything from his job, insurance, bills, establishing all aspects of our lives in preparation of him being deployed. He was sent to Paris Island, South Carolina for staging and preparation to enter another country. His deployment to Iraq became a reality in December of 1990. At this time, I was four months pregnant.I was praying so hard for nothing to happen to him and for the Lord to help me survive if I had to raise this child on my own. Aaron was praying for God to keep him safe so he could return home to see his baby.You see, she was not only strength for me to keep going but she also gave him strength to fight harder."

"The next few months were very hard; as much as you didn't want to think about death, it was still in the back of your mind. Even so, I felt a close walk with the Lord."

"In January, as the Gulf War (Desert Storm) came into full swing, it was touch and go for us until the invasion was over. A few weeks after the invasion into Iraq, he was able to call home. He had survived the invasion which was another miracle and what a relief it was for both of us!"

"As my due date was approaching, my doctor advised me to get a pediatrician because the baby was in the breech position. On April 24, 1991, my last doctor's exam before my due date, I went to meet my pediatrician to keep her on standby for when the baby was born. Later that evening, the phone rang and it was Aaron, saying he was back in Saudi Arabia and they were talking about sending him home in a few weeks. He said, "I have some bad news. We've had an indefinite stay. I might not make it home before the baby is born." We were both a little discouraged, but later that evening, I went to bed and prayed, "Lord, if he's not going to make it home then let me go ahead and have this baby." Again, God honored my prayer and my water broke at 4:00 am the next morning. The next miracle that happened was throughout the birthing process. I experienced no labor pains and our daughter was born at 5:54 am on April 25th, 1991. She was breech and also had jaundice. At that time, having a C-section meant it had to be done in an operating room. It was serious surgery. Because she had jaundice, they carried her into the nursery to care for her for several hours. Aaron and I had not yet decided on a name for her, so for now, she would be, Baby Butler. When I finally settled in a room, my family had gathered where we received the 'phone call from heaven!' I had not spoken to Aaron since the day before, when everything was fine and the baby was not due for two more weeks. He was unaware that I had given birth to our daughter. He had called my work and they told him I was in the hospital. Somehow the call came directly to my hospital room and I saw they were bringing my baby girl to my room for the first time since she had been born. See how God works? His plan placed us together by telephone so we could share this special moment together. We named

Aaron Butler with baby Shelby

her together and our baby girl is now known as Shelby Marlene Butler. The miracles just kept happening because Aaron was able to come home safely three weeks from the day she was born."

"Things appeared to be getting back to normal for a while but then there seemed to be a lot of tension and arguments between the two of us. His absence, the effects of the war, the independence of not having anyone to answer to, all played a major role in what was about to happen next. The arguments got worse and we agreed we did not want to end up hating each other, so we agreed to separate for a while. He got an apartment but every day he stopped by to see Shelby. He loved her so much! We also loved each other but the fighting was unbearable. We both had remained faithful during the separation. We never wanted to dishonor each other by being unfaithful. I visited Aaron at his place often. I begged him to come home and try to make our marriage work. I just needed to make our marriage work. I just needed my family together no matter what! During one of our visits, I conceived our son, Jarrod Michael Butler. God knew Aaron's heart and that he would do the right thing by his family and return home when he found out I was pregnant."

"Within a week, my family was restored and even though the road gets rough at times, we weather the storms now as a family. These were all miracles that God worked through for the Butler family. He not only has a plan; He has a purpose. Your family is worth fighting for. It may seem easy to walk away but the right thing to do is to stay and let God work it out. Place your trust in God and let Him guide you because greater is He that is in you, than he that is in the world." [Lisa Butler].

11. ASSISTANT PASTOR ~
CAGNEY TANNER.

Recently the First Full Gospel Church had a revival that lasted longer than most. God wasn't ready to close it down at the week's end, so it continued with the anointed power of the Holy Ghost. What was really unusual about this revival was the evangelist. He preached about heaven so glorious you wanted to reach up and take your place around the throne. He preached hell so hot you could smell the stench of the

Assistant Pastor
Cagney Tanner

brimstone. This was old time holiness preaching talked about by your grandparents, ('back in my day.') There was no ear tickling but some heavy duty toe stepping was going on, and when your toes get stepped on by an anointed man of God, it won't take long for the altars to line up, and they did! Men, women, and children came and filled the pews night after night to hear the old-time preacher man who happened to be, in fact, a 23 year old Georgia evangelist, raised by holiness parents.

We liked him so much, we decided to keep him; he liked us so much, he agreed to stay and become our Assistant Pastor. He has moved into the parsonage in Lake City, Florida, but he will never be alone in Lake City. The young men at the church have all 'adopted' him as their big brother. As wonderful as our young men are (this should come as no big surprise), Assistant Pastor Cagney Tanner has preferred the company of another young member at the First Full Gospel Church, Shelby Marlene

Cagney & Shelby

Butler, daughter of Aaron and Lisa Butler. Shelby and Cagney seem to enjoy each other's company and it appears to be the 'match made in heaven.'

Brother Cagney, I probably don't need to draw your attention to this, but just to be on the safe side, I offer this bit of advice... "Shelby is a beautiful young woman with the singing voice of an angel, and... a great Big Daddy named Aaron, who treasures his Baby Girl. So be aware...be very aware!

I know Cagney is a God fearing, Bible-believing man of God, so I said, "Brother if you could reach thousands of people with a single message, what would that message be?" This is his message from Mark 5:25-34, entitled 'Don't Stop Until You Get There!'

"A certain woman has an issue of blood in her life. The Bible said she went to every doctor and spent all her money. Instead of getting better, she got worse. There was one thing about this woman ~ she was not going to stop until she got what she needed in her body! A lot of people stop short of their miracle, but for us to ever get where we need to be we are going to have to ...NOT...stop. This certain woman got her miracle by NOT stopping but going ALL

Bro. Cagney Tanner & Pastor Stanley Ellis baptizing at the First Full Gospel Church baptistery in Lake City, Florida. Praising God for Baptism by Emersion ~ An External Act of an Internal Change! The Sinful Man is Buried ~ A Child of God Is Risen!

THE WAY to the miracle! You may have a lot of things in your life that needs a miracle in it. If you will press all the way through and NOT stop, Jesus has your miracle! When you take a trip out of town, you're never going to get to the place you are going if you stop. So to get there, you can't stop! You've got to keep going! When the five hundred in the Bible were given a choice to stay in Bethany or go to Jerusalem, only some went to Jerusalem because they had a desire NOT to stop but to go all the way! Whatever you do, as children of God, we must pray we never lose our desire to go all the way through!" [Assistant Pastor Cagney Tanner]

12. SHELBY MARLENE BUTLER

She has been mentioned many times and her picture has been posted on two different testimonies. She is a precious sister with an angel's voice! Her testimony is: "Since I was very young, I have believed and trusted in God. He has never left nor failed me. When I was four years old, I preached a message to about twenty-five people but the Holy Spirit spoke through me. Life is not always easy but I continue to trust and serve the Lord. God is my first love, my true love; there is no one else like Him. I never took drugs, drank or smoked because God has always been by my side. I intend to serve Him for the rest of my life; I owe my life to Him. He gave His life for me. No one else could ever do that! His love is unconditional. Like the song says, 'Nobody Can Do Me Like Jesus!'

There were times in my life when I felt alone! I felt like saying, 'God, where are You?' but each time He was faithful, and showed up right on time! I'm not perfect, but I am forgiven and, because of His precious blood He shed at Calvary, was able to be born again, set free! If we just trust Him, and allow Him to take control of our lives, He will make a way for us, as He said , 'Seek ye first the kingdom of God and all these things will be added unto you.' Joshua 1:9 says, 'Have I not commanded thee? Be strong and of good courage; be not afraid neither be thou dismayed: for the Lord thy God is with thee withersoever thou goest.' The Lord has blessed me with a gift of singing, by His grace. He is not through working with us, for He molds us to improve us for our walk with Him. Trust in God. He has proven He will never let you down. God is my everything. He is all I need." [Shelby Butler]

13. MARY ANDREWS

Recently, the congregation of First Full Gospel Church was realizing a unique answer to prayer: We prayed, Lord build our church! Fill these church pews and pack this sanctuary with worshippers from wall to wall. Then a young couple announced they were going to be parents! Then another was expecting their baby in August, and another, and another, and soon we knew we needed to open up a nice nursery for all the beautiful new babies! That's when we found Mary. With her soft voice, easy smile and her gentle touch, she was perfect! The babies have accepted her as their very own teacher, and we love her! She has had little chance to leave the nursery to give her personal testimony; she even watches the church service on the television

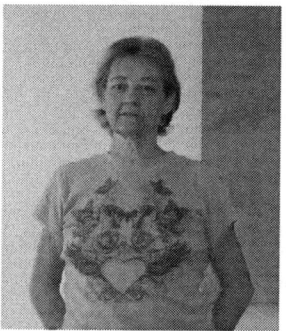

Mary Andrews

monitor in the nursery. I am honored to present her testimony here:

"My name is Mary Andrews and I have been an alcoholic all my life. In April of 1996, I moved to Florida to take care of my mother. I turned my addiction to alcohol over to God, completely. He delivered me from my alcoholism in January of 1997. I have never taken a drink since the Lord healed me. I also was troubled with smoking. I started smoking in 1970 but January, 2008, I asked God to heal my smoking addiction. Again He answered my prayer. God did it and I give Him all the praise!" [Mary Andrews]

14. SUE COLLINS

I met Sue Collins when she was married to Vernon Collins. He recently passed away and we lost a dear friend we loved but in fact, Vernon was ready to see Jesus. The angels didn't grieve because they welcomed him home! Sue's heart was breaking as she made the funeral plans for her husband, but being a Christian, she knew He would be waiting for her in heaven.

Sue Collins

Sue is a giver, one of those people who seeks out ways to be nice to others. She has been hired by families to take care of their loved ones and it has always been an additional comfort to know she believes in prayer, and with good reason. When her daughter was just a little girl, she was ill, but the doctors offered her no help. So Sue took her to 'Dr. Jesus' and received complete restoration. Her faith has increased over the years but in the early months of 2008, she began to feel stress and fatigue due to family problems. She decided to talk seriously with God. What was she doing wrong? She was still serving God... but she was hindered by dwelling on fears and worries. Being submissive to Him, willing to obey His call, she reached a new level of understanding with God. She had received miracles! Surely, she should pray with others and show them God is able! He proved to her He was the Healer. Now she was needed to pray and actively lay hands on the sick and watch them recover. What a blessing! [Sue Collins]

15. EUNICE DAVENPORT

She is a very unique individual. I could spend hours listening to her down-home stories. She can tell you how to cure almost any illness with which you may be dealing . She knows about herbs and she knows about hard times. She can recall the time when raising a family had nothing to do with wants, just needs, but all those lean years have taught her something very important: how to lean on God. She knows how to get the prayer wheel turning and she knows Who made the wheel she just turned! It's all about God! Sister Eunice has this to say about God: "I know God has kept His hand on me and my children. I had experiences in my life I know was the result of God's intervention! He has also healed my son, Morris, at a tent meeting! I'm so thankful to God for keeping me and my kids safe. I praise God for it all!"

Eunice Davenport

Eunice was married to Lawrence Bascum Albritton. Eunice has two children, Morris and Katrina; both of them have accepted Jesus Christ. Morris is a contractor and Katrina works in home care. Katrina has a gift for teaching and ministering God's Word. Katrina is married to Harvey Hester, who is also a Pentecostal preacher in addition to his secular job with the State of Florida. Eunice can praise God forever for the sweet peace that comes from knowing her children are willingly safe in the arms of Jesus.

16. HARVEY AND KATRINA (ALBRITTON) HESTER

They are as different as day and night, in some ways, but in the way they choose to serve God, they are in total agreement. Harvey Hester is a man who is proud of his Texas roots. He preaches while telling about the times and places that were precious to him. He has a brother who is also in the ministry, but when Harvey talks about 'Sam,' his eyes start to dance! He looks up to Sam! No one does it better than Sam whether it's preaching or southern gospel, according to little brother Harvey, so when Harvey's stamp of approval is applied, you 'done good.' Harvey's preaching is simply a combination of Word of God authority (ya'll can take it to the bank), and homespun stories of "I remember when." Then the guitars come out and Harvey is no longer in the forefront. Suddenly, the man of

Harvey & Katrina Hester

God sings those old gospel greats and you know the angels stop to listen. Harvey never learned to sing from his diaphragm. He just sings straight from the heart and the Spirit rejoices, but he doesn't even seem to know how important his music ministry really is. I know Harvey uses his music to carry himself to higher places with God. He has always just 'picked' a song he likes to sing, unaware of how many more could be blessed by his anointed singing, if given the chance. Since Brother Harvey likes stories, I thought I would toss this one his way:

Years ago in Montana, an old woman lived in a cabin. The winter winds blew and the blizzards came and the poor old woman had nary a penny to her name to buy food to stay alive. An old miner saw the smoke from her chimney and stopped to warm his hands and feet. She, as was the custom, invited him in and fixed him a hot cup of coffee as she apologized for having no food to serve her guest. He looked around the small cabin and saw how destitute she really was and said a prayer for her. She was very grateful to the man, (who obviously was sent by God) and said, 'I have no food but I see your hands get very cold as you travel through this land, so I will give you something to help you. She pulled out a rock from under her bed and said, 'I heat this rock every night and keep it close to me to keep me warm. I'd like for you to have it.' The old gold miner extended his hand to receive her gift, but then he stopped, 'Dear woman, do you not know this rock is the purest gold in the land? It's worth a king's ransom!' She looked at him and replied, 'All I know, is it really keeps you warm on cold Montana nights.' (Harvey, have you thought about the 'rock' you've had all these years? There's a whole world out there who could use your gold.)

Katrina is 'cut from the same cloth' as her mama. She's a hard working southern girl who expects only what she earns, nothing more and nothing less, but God evaluates job performance differently than the world does. God rewards Katrina openly, not with a paycheck, but with His love and His anointing. When Katrina speaks about her Lord, you know she's walked with Him, up close and personal. Katrina doesn't know any other way. It's hard for her to understand why some say, 'I need a touch.' She could never be satisfied with just a touch. She cries out, "Lord, fill me up with Your glory. I need to walk through Your Living Waters, feel that stirring deep inside my soul that makes me shout out Your name, the name above all others… Jesus, Glorious Jesus!"

When she prays for you, she holds you lovingly as she petitions the throne of God to send angels to minister to you, and right then you know, He already has, for angels are messengers of God, and Katrina (Albritton) Hester is indeed a messenger of God. I have experienced Katrina's anointing first-hand.

She is the kind of person who has church wherever she goes. When she comes to visit, everything else takes a back seat because we are going to get down and talk about our favorite subject …the Lord. 'Boy, ain't this a beautiful day' will all at once become…' I can see God loves His children, blessing us with this glorious sunshine.' A cloudy day doesn't stop us, 'Lord let the rains come and the harvests be bountiful!' She always has a word of praise right on the tip of her tongue.

This is her own testimony: "We lived in Texas for 15 years until we moved back to Lake City, Florida where I was born and raised. We had been going to lots of different churches, but there are none like the First Full Gospel Church. I believe it was God's timing and His Will for us to be here, and we are blessed to have such a wonderful Spirit- filled church. God dwells there! Many wonderful people worship here and that's where I want to be, where God will always be praised!" [Katrina 'Albritton' Hester]

17. VIRGINIA TINER

This lady is a very special child of God. Her smile can light up the darkest room and her compassion for others is unsurpassed. She looks after her family with her last ounce of strength. She places others' needs above her own and God saw He must take her under His wings if she were to survive. I call her 'Sister', Father calls her 'His.' This is her testimony: "In 1972, I lost my son and I was overcome with grief. Each day was just a reminder he was gone and I was about to think, 'I can't go on!' I was struggling on my own, my tortured mind trying to make sense of my life. My hope was gone; I was so depressed my body just shut down, exhausted. I

Virginia Tiner & Shelby
(Granddaughter)

thought I had all my problems labeled, then family problems cropped up, but God rescued me."

"In 2004, I got saved at First Full Gospel Church. I felt like God elevated my soul to a place I had never reached in my life! There was such a peaceful release that came over me, as though I had wings that allowed me to soar, but it was the power of God, winds of His Spirit, beneath me that lifted me even higher! It strengthened me to know He died on the Cross for ME. I know with His help, all things are possible. He comes first in my life and I love Him with all my heart. My daily prayer is, 'Give me more of You, Lord.' Each day I strive, making sure He stays first in my life."

18. BILL AND BETTY FOE

When I first met them, I was aware the two of them were more than just husband and wife, they were good friends. They share a good life and also an awesome God. Bill is retired, but not from serving God. Bill loves to walk in the early morning and he chooses to walk indoors at our local Walmart store. The moment I walk through the doors of the store (I'm shopping; he's walking), I see his smile. It's almost as if someone told him a really good joke and he's withholding the punch line. He has accepted me as a sister in the Lord, and I get crazy urges sometimes to do silly things to bring a smile to someone's face. I think he is just waiting to see what I'll do next, but his smile is reward enough. On Mondays at 1:00 pm, our church doors

Betty & Bill Foe

are open wide for anyone who wants to pray or to be prayed for. One of the most reliable prayer warriors we have is Bill Foe, but he doesn't limit himself to the church. Once I was in Walmart and he could tell I wasn't feeling well. A very humble, soft-spoken man walked up to me and said, "Would it be okay if I prayed for you right here?" I knew Bill Foe had just walked down the aisle where I had been shopping. I told him to pray right now, right here. I know what prayer can do! When Bill Foe prays, heaven and earth will be moved to see his requests get answered. Keep on praying, Brother Bill!

Sister Betty is a caregiver by occupation, but she is a people-lover by nature. Of course, her nature is spiritual, and her love is the love of God. She is drawn to anyone who needs to talk, cry, pray or just needs a big hug. She's a tiny woman but her capacity for caring goes far beyond her petite stature; it reaches heaven's gates! Her prayers have legs. That sounds odd, but you'd have to meet her to understand. If someone prays with her who may need a job, she doesn't leave him at the altar. She helps with his resume. If someone needs answers from Social Security, Sister Betty makes phone calls. That's why I say her prayers have legs. Sometimes it's hard enough to get someone to care enough to say a heartfelt prayer, but the Foes are an exceptional couple. They know how to pray and get results. Sister Betty follows up and makes sure all her little prayer sayers are nice and safely tucked in, because if they aren't secure, feeling like someone truly cares for them, then she's not happy either. She's like a mother hen with her little chicks making sure all God's little ones are taken care of. That's Sister Betty Foe. When I asked them to give me their testimony, together they gave me II Timothy 2:15 that states in the KJV, "Study to shew thyself approved unto God, a workman that needeth not to be ashamed, rightly dividing the word of truth." This is the only way to be fulfilled in your Christian walk. The pastor calls for prayer requests and the Foes reply, "We have unsaved children and loved ones." I know this was not meant for our ears, but God's ; "just a reminder, Lord, we are waiting for Your perfect timing for their salvation!" With a smile, they sit back in their pew and wait for God's blessing in their family, assured it will come and so will He!

19. MAY JUNE SIMMONS

This is a strong woman of God. Her faith has seen her through trials in her life that would make some question God, but I have never seen her doubt the Lord. May June has a beautiful name, (two in fact) that she carries with her with pride, and she should be proud. God chose these two months of the year to show beautiful flowers and warm, balmy days. May June exudes her warmth, and there are no flowers on earth that compare with her beautiful spirit. She is married to (Bruce) James Simmons, mother to Lisa Butler and grandmother to Shelby and Jarrod Butler, who attend First Full Gospel. May June submitted the picture of her baptism, which took place in 2000. with her testimony: "The first time I came to the First Full Gospel Church, I was broke. Our house pump had gone out and we had no money to fix it. I was crying and went to the altar to get prayer. When I got home, a man was there who owed my husband $2000 for work he had done. He paid him $1500 of it, and we got our pump fixed. I didn't come to church regularly,

May June Simmon's Baptism

because I was caregiver to my sick mother, member of the Church of Christ. She believed I wouldn't get to heaven unless I was baptized. I wasn't baptized until 2000. My mother passed away in 1977. The Lord delivered me from smoking in February of 2006. I believe it took that long because I had smoked for forty-seven years! If He can deliver ME from the cigarette addiction, I know He can take it away from you, too!" [May June Simmons]

20. MELVIN AND MARY ANN KIRBY

The Kirbys have been attending First Full Gospel for about 16 years. Melvin Kirby is one of our Trustees. Mary Ann is a licensed minister with the Living Word of Faith. A few years ago, the Lord told Sister Mary Ann to start the 1:00 pm Monday prayer meeting and she obeyed. From the beginning, the seekers came in. At first, there were just a few; then as word got out that prayers were being answered, the sick were being healed, and God was blessing His children, the attendance grew... and the anointing was stronger in the other services. Mary Ann gave this for her testimony: " Since we have started at the First Full Gospel Church, we have seen miracles and God is

Melvin & Mary Ann Kirby

really pouring out His Spirit in nearly all our services, but the most important thing is we are seeing people saved! If I was preaching to 10,000 people, I would have to say, 'If you are not saved, ask Jesus to come into your heart. John 3:16 says, 'For God so loved the world, He gave His only begotten Son, that whosoever believeth in Him, should not perish, but have everlasting life.' The Bible says, TODAY is the day of salvation. Don't put it off until tomorrow, God never promised us a tomorrow." [Mary Ann Kirby]

21. CHRIS AND VICKI SINGLETON AND FAMILY

The Singletons are a Christian couple who built their home on the foundation of Jesus Christ. There is no doubt He is the Decision Maker in their family. Vicki is Melvin and Mary Ann Kirby's daughter. It's plain to see why they are so proud of this family. Chris is a Christian Dad who follows the teachings of the Word and emulates his Heavenly Father. He treasures God's gift of his wife, Vicki, and two beautiful daughters, Katherine Grace and Victoria. Vicki is a mother who learned to pray at an early age. She recognizes the Spirit's call and walks in His grace. This is Vicki's own testimony: "We are thankful for God's many blessings, faithfulness, and grace. He shows His love to us in many ways, every day. When we look into our children's eyes, we see His tenderness. When we watch the sun set or rise, we see His magnificence and creativity.

Front L-R: Katherine Grace, Chris & Victoria. Mom Vicki is standing

When our prayers are answered and our needs are met, we feel His presence. We are privileged to be called His children." [Vicki Singleton] When the Kirbys say their prayers at night, I am very sure their hearts are filled with adoration for a God so loving He sent them a child to carry on the old covenant, the promise of the Father to be their God and they would be His people.

22. BETTY HALTIWANGER

When the church doors open, Betty Haltewanger comes breezing in, full of excitement as she anticipates what just might happen tonight. She knows God will speak to her heart because she has a willingness to listen and that is all it takes. This is her testimony: "As a child, church wasn't a part of my life, mostly due to no transportation. I married at 14 years of age and by the time I was 20, I had three daughters and a son.

God chose to take my son home when he was just 14 months old. Through tears of grief, my husband and I could not see God working out our salvation through his death. I was tormented by nightmares, seeing my baby boy sitting on his grave, crying and reaching for me, begging me to save Him from that dark place. I was hardly sleeping at all and one day I decided to start going to church. My husband came with me and

Betty Haltiwanger

heard the preacher say we could see our son again in heaven, if we were saved. We gave our hearts to Jesus that day back in 1962. I no longer had the tormenting dreams, but a vision of heaven's gates protecting hundreds of infants and toddlers as they cooed and giggled in delight, playing in the sparkling water that danced in fountains of Gloryland! My son was in the midst and he was the happiest of all, but 15 years later, God watched as I drifted into the world. I was driving drunk on the freeways of Houston, Texas, losing my way home, but God took control and brought me back safe and fully redeemed. Praise God!" [Betty Haltiwanger]

23. MONTA POITEVINT

She is the sister of Betty (Poitevint) Boston, and she's an independent woman who loves God and family, and treasures all her friends. She has a real gusto for life. Before she retired, she managed a paint store (Sherwin Williams), but even that doesn't

nearly describe how good she was at her job. She could see a color and match it perfectly. I looked forward to her testimony and this is what she had to say: "I thank God for all His guidance throughout my entire life. As I look back, I see God's reasons

Monta with son and wife

for leading me down my paths of ups and downs. I realized His special gift He gave me, the desire to climb higher and prosper as I climbed. He blessed me with two sons and my love for them is beyond compare! He knew I had a compassionate heart, so He gave me a job where I could mentor my young employees and customers."

Monta & Betty

"When my health began to fail, I had to dig deep inside to search for my Lord and the blessings came. God was the first to give me hope and confidence. He has touched my life from head to toe. He has given me His peace and understanding as I wait for the plan He has for my life. All fear and doubts are gone, replaced by God. I came to this church years ago with my mother and sister. I will never forget it and I'm glad to be back." [Monta Poitevint]

24. MIKE AND BETTY PARKER

They have been members in the First Full Gospel Church since 1984. Sister Betty Parker is a lady with a heart too big for words. She is compassionate, sincere and quick to reach out to the broken-hearted. She has no capacity for prejudice or intolerance. She likes things simple so she just loves everybody and prays for them, too.

Brother Mike is a scholar and thrives on studying the Word of God. He has served as Choir leader and adult Sunday School teacher. He excels at whatever he does. Sister Betty taught Sunday School and was a role model for the girls in the congregation. She exemplifies a woman who humbly loves God. This is the testimony from Brother Mike Parker: "God is seen in all

Mike & Betty Parker

His handy work; the heavens, the universe, the cosmose, the stars, the earth, all creatures created and even in childbirth, where the first breath is taken, and down to the everyday decisions we make. He gave His only son for our salvation: "for God so loved the world that

He gave His only begotten son, that whosoever believeth in Him should not perish but have everlasting life." (John 3:16). Therefore, as His creation, we will not have an excuse at the Judgment day that we didn't hear about Jesus. We will stand before God without excuse. I pray you will accept Jesus as your personal savior before that final judgment day." [Mike Parker]

25. ANGEL AND GLORIA MARTINEZ

I met the Martinez family through God in a very unique way. In 1999, we had just finalized the paperwork on the home God had blessed to us. We wanted to paint our house and searched weeks for a handyman for the job, but each time someone came up, I turned him down. I just believed this home was a gift from God and I was particular about who touched it. One painter put out his cigarette, grinding it into the grass. Another reeked of alcohol, but had excellent references. I said no to both of them. My husband was feeling frustrated when he said, 'You know we can't get an angel to do this work, don't you?' but, I needed more time. The next day, I

Gloria & Angel Martinez

called a pastor we knew and asked if he knew someone who could do the job. His choice …'Angel' Martinez. That night we found an 'angel' to work on God's house. We loved God's little joke. He has a great sense of humor! Angel said he played drums at First Full Gospel Church. Gloria keeps a prayer list and honors them. Here are their testimonies: "Jesus is the same yesterday, today, and forever. I got saved at 8 years of age and now, 52 years later, I can say He is STILL the same today, yesterday and forever. He walks with me, talks with me, and lives in me. Thank you, Jesus!" [Gloria Martinez] Angel is a man of few words, but they are from his heart, "In 1973, Jesus came into my life. He changed my life and I am a different person. Many times He helps me and heals my body." [Angel Martinez]

26. LLOYD AND PAT MILLER

Some people attend church, but others, like the Millers, adopt the congregation as family, loving and always praying for them. These are truly two special friends from God. Here is Pat's testimony: "Have you ever prayed and God showed you a promise and you knew it was from God? Let me tell you about my promise from God: One day I was sitting on the beach in North Carolina. I was heartbroken because my children were drinking and doing drugs but they were all raised knowing about God and living a good life. I started to go to church but instead

Pat & Lloyd Miller

I went to the beach, knowing I would find peace there. I sat down on a board and looked down at the Lindy Star ring my children gave me one Christmas, and while I talked to God, I saw the setting had become all stars! I knew they were going to be okay. That was 30 years ago, and I still claimed that promise as I watched two of my sons come to God. I know God's not done yet; I have one more son out in the world. So I expect a miracle any day! God blessed me with a Christian step-daughter with a good husband and two handsome little boys. I can't forget Kelly, my precious daughter-in-law. Just weeks ago, God confirmed His promise He was bringing in my family circle and it is just as He said. So don't give up on God. He's always right on time! My husband and I attend First Full Gospel in Lake City, Florida, and we love the Lord. We thank Him for His many blessings." [Pat Miller]

27. PRENTICE AND DOROTHY HARDEN

The Harden family are very precious to First Full Gospel Church. Prentice Harden is a trustee on the board and with his wife, Dorothy, they are a great spiritual team! Brother Prentice is a Bible scholar and he loves the book of Revelation. He has armed himself with the Sword of the Lord and he's ready to do combat with the enemy! One strategic plan is to increase his forces, winning more soldiers for the

Lord's service. He is known for his fervent plea to anyone lost in sin… don't wait! There isn't time! The rapture is just outside your door and Jesus Christ is knocking that you might be saved before those Eastern skies divide!

This is a word from Brother Prentice Harden: "For God so loved the world that He gave His only begotten Son that whosoever believeth in Him should not perish but have everlasting life." (John 3:16).

The Hardens - Cindy, Prentice, Dorothy, Emory & Ann

"Jesus shed His blood for the remission of our sins. He died for us so we don't have to face the second death. Jesus said, "If you love me, keep my commandments." I love God with all my heart, soul and mind. Jesus is the only Way! Salvation is the most important thing in this life; I must study the Bible to know God's Will and be approved unto God." [Prentice Harden]

The gentler half of the Harden couple is Sister Dorothy Harden. This picture was taken many years ago; their hair was dark (and plentiful). The best compliment to give a married couple is that they are the best of

Dorothy & Prentice Harden

friends. She is proud of the man she calls 'Prinny" and his eyes still light up when she walks into the room. That is something of which to be proud. Sister 'Dot' has a special place in the hearts of our small congregation because she worships God unashamedly and her voice reverberates through the sanctuary … and God is pleased, but she is also noted for another talent. Pastor Ellis' mouth waters as he tells all about Dot's famous 'Nanner Puddin' and she never lets him down when we have our 'dinners on the grounds.' Sister Dot loves the song, 'It's a Grand and Glorious Feeling.' With that in mind, she says,

'Nanner Puddin' Lady

"I would like to thank God for the blood of the Lord Jesus Christ and everlasting life. I believe in the Virgin birth of the Son of the Living

God, Jesus Christ, who died on the cross, but Praise God He is risen and ascended to the Father, and He's coming back for His own any day now! Now that's the Grand and Glorious Feeling I'm waiting for!" [Dorothy Harden]

28. JACK AND FRAN HUDSON

They recently celebrated their fiftieth wedding anniversary and celebrated it at the church with their family and their church family. Jack has a slow smile that grows very serious when you talk about the Lord, and Fran, or 'Granny Frannie' as she is called by their family, walks with the Lord, day and night. Brother Jack had this to say for his testimony: "My wife, Fran, and I both grew up attending Sunday School and church at

Fran & Jack Hudson

First Assembly of God in Bessemer, Alabama. We got married shortly after I returned from the Army. We raised our three boys in the same church we grew up in, continuing to be involved in activities as a family. A job change in 1972, led us to Lake City, Florida. Shortly after moving, we went to First Assembly of God in Lake City on Sunday and met Melvin and Mary Ann Kirby. Thirty-six years later, we are still friends. My new job kept me busy and sometimes I missed church on Sunday to work at home. After a while, I drifted away from God and I stopped going to church at all. Since I had pulled away, Fran eventually stopped going to church, too. By now, the boys were older, making their own decisions. I stayed away from church for 15 or 20 years. Fran went at times and tried to talk me into going back, but I said I was too busy and not interested. One day in my travels, the Lord allowed me to see a little country church that stirred my heart. I told Fran I might be considering going back to church and she agreed to go with me if I did, but like most good intentions, I didn't follow up on them. Mary Ann Kirby and Melvin were still close to us and every time Mary Ann left our home, she said, "Jack, I want to see you in church tomorrow!" To which I replied, as usual, "O.K., save me a seat and I'll be there." We both knew I had no intention of going, but after I retired, I felt God tug a little harder at my heart to find a church. I told Fran I thought we should try the Kirby's church since they had been inviting us for so long. On Saturday night, the Kirbys were over for a visit and Mary Ann made her usual remark, wanting to see me in church tomorrow. I made my usual comeback remark, but the next morning I entered their church and sat down next to them and watched Mary Ann smile from ear to ear! When I entered the First Full Gospel Church, I knew I felt the Holy Spirit. There was a feeling of love that seemed to

Fran & Jack Hudson Family Photo

permeate the entire congregation. I told Fran, "I don't have to look any further. I found where I want to be. The pastor and all the people are friendly, genuine and caring." This was the place I could start over with God. The pastor once mentioned 'second chances,' and it stayed with me . A lot of us have turned away from God, but His love and compassion gives us a second chance. I thank my Savior daily for my second chance." [Jack Hudson]

29. LINDA (VARNES) LARSON

Linda is a returning member to First Full Gospel and she is as excited to be back as we are to have her back. She is an unusually gifted woman who never hesitates to offer help wherever it is needed. The Lord calls her name, and she says, "Yes," not, "Why?" May that be our example! This is her testimony: "My name is Linda (Varnes) Larson. I am 56 and glad to say I am back home where I belong. I was raised in the First Full Gospel Church. We lived in Watertown, next to Southern Woods Mill off Washington Street, which is now Varnes Road. I left when I was 17. I remember the old piano and the wooden benches. I still remember Brother

Linda (Varnes) Larson

Alvie Boston as pastor forever. We were almost kin through marriages

of his son, George, to my aunt (my dad's sister, Jeanette Varnes). My cousin, Charles Finley married his daughter, Linda. I can remember Ulis Taylor becoming pastor later. The church grew quickly with our families like the Browns, the Greens, the Robinsons, the Hardens, the Varnes, the Taylors, the Sanders, the Clyatts, the Williams, the Powells, Albrittons, and many more! The special singing was pretty good with groups like the trio of Glenda Williams (Richardson), Susan Moates (Albritton) and me. The Brown family sang along with Brother Ulis Taylor, Billy

Vera & Alva Boston

Earl Sanders, and Brother Charles Clyatt. We sure had fun! There were camp meetings and youth rallies and you couldn't keep us away! Revivals at the church had preachers like Randy Hobbs, Little David Smith, and Brother Al Jones, who could preach Holy Ghost and fire down. When you were in their services, you knew you had been to church! The Spirit I felt back then is still alive in this church today, because I have felt the touch from the Spirit of God."

Ulis Taylor, Charles Clyatt and Billy Earl Sanders

"As we grow older, we seem to naturally slip away to our own ventures. I lost a dear friend when Glenda Williams passed away, and some pastors have come and gone. Pastor Stan Ellis and his wife, Peaches, are precious to us and we hope they stay on for a long time. Three weeks before my husband grew ill, I rededicated my life to God and I wanted to return to my home church very badly. My husband, Robert Wendell Larson, passed away on September 4th, 2008, and God saw fit to ease me back with my church family here to help me deal with my loss. My emptiness is gone and although many of my old friends are not here now, their memories will remain forever. I thank God for such a loving church that welcomes the downtrodden back with open arms. I pray I will be an influence for one who seeks God's mercy and love." [Linda Varnes Larson]

30. LOREE AND ROGER WIDNEY

Recently, the First Full Gospel Church has been seeing the pews fill up as the Spirit has been blessing the services each week. One couple who came to be a part of our family of God was the Widneys. They were an instant match with the congregation. Loree is more reserved than Roger, but she has a quick smile and gentle spirit. Roger is a man with a sense of humor. He's first in line to offer help. They have already shown their charity and compassion by helping with youth projects. Mentioning 'Goldtimers' brings a quick smile from Roger and Loree. It seems they enjoy the antics of 'Granny,' a skit character created

Loree and Roger Widney

for the 50's group, which meets in the Fellowship Hall seasonally. Wherever you see the Widneys, you can expect a good time. They bring joy wherever they go. We love them! Roger offered this as his testimony: "We firmly believe in tithing and prayer works! Loree and I had our previous homes paid for and upon getting married June 7th , 2008, sought God's will in purchasing a newer home. We prayed that if it was His will, He would make a way, even though we were in a declining housing market. Her home sold on August 2nd, 2008 and we bought our new home on August 13, 2008, with a mortgage. By the time the first payment was due, my home had sold. We were able to pay off the new home. Praise be to God!" [Loree and Roger Widney]

31. CHARLES AND BECKY GETZ

Charles W. Getz is a former pastor of the First Full Gospel Church where he served from March of 1994 through March of 1998. He and his wife, Elsia Rebecca (Becky) Getz were loved by many of the members. When Pastor Getz preached his sermons, one member recalls they were always anointed messages. He loved to study God's Word. Sister Becky

Charles & Becky Getz

has recently passed away after a lingering illness, but many said she fought the good fight and her compassionate God healed her by way of heaven.

32. TOMMIE AND FRAN RICHARDSON

If you see Sister Fran, she has a smile. Brother Tommie offers a warm embrace. First Full Gospel is called a loving church and these folks are just one reason. Tommie gave this testimony: "God has been so good to me! He gave me a great family, wife and children. I had a mini stroke and was out of work for awhile. God put me to my knees where He told

Tommie & Fran Richardson

me He would take care of me in His time. He hasn't stopped blessing me since!" [Tommie Richardson]

33. EARL B. AND CAROLYN BRADY

When Watertown was booming, the family name 'Brady,' was very familiar, as it is today. Recently a meeting with the Bradys resulted in getting answers to many of my questions as well as some old photos that visually carried me back to the past. As we spoke, I was moved by a testimony by Mrs. Brady. She had this to say: " I was told of a job that was opening at a local hospital, working in the dietary field. At first I hesitated because I had no formal education to qualify me, but I was urged to apply. The interviewer said the requirements were pretty strict. It almost made me

Bud & Carolyn Brady

want to give up, but then I heard the urging of God and He said I should do this. At first the job was going to require I work weekends but, as I checked further, I saw the hours had been set to give me Sunday mornings off for church. God knew what He was doing. I got the job!"

Bud Brady offers these words of advice: "When you come to God, keep an open mind because God wants to talk to you. If your heart is right with God and your mind is open, you can hear His message to you. He is a loving God and He wants to guide you, but we have to stop sometimes, be still and listen for Him to speak. Sometimes He speaks and gives signs we might miss if we don't keep our minds open. He uses many ways of getting through to you. You can believe it's God's way." [Bud Brady]

34. BILL AND MINNIE LEE WALLIN

This couple has a long history of covenant acts with Jesus Christ, for many years. Minnie Lee is very proud of her Christian heritage, recorded here with her own mother's legacy: Hattie Lee Register was born on September 22nd, 1930 to John Houston (1888 - 1958) and Minnie Register (1893 - 1950) They were poor share-croppers who spent their lives in Lake City, Florida until they passed away. They are buried at the Oak Grove Cemetery in Deep Creek. Hattie Lee remembered her father, John, had a crippling disease all her life.

Bill & Minnie Lee Wallin

In the early 1940's, Hattie Lee worked as a waitress at the bus station in town. One day, a sailor walked into the restaurant and into her life. Raymond C. Hill was in the U.S. Navy, stationed at Watertown, Florida. When he met Hattie Lee, the young Baptist girl of his dreams, he asked her to marry him. In January of 1945, Hattie Lee Register became Hattie Lee (Register) Hill, his wife. Their first child, Minnie Lee was born in December of 1945.

One day in 1946, Hattie Lee, her mother (Minnie Lee Register), and a friend of Hattie Lee's decided to go to a revival at the little church across the railroad tracks, the Congregational Holiness Church. Rev. John Dortch was the pastor. That night, Hattie Lee felt as though the preacher was talking just to her. The Spirit was so strong! Hattie Lee knew her friend must be feeling the same stirring in her heart, but her friend wasn't the one moved by the Spirit, but

Hattie Lee herself. She knew she was already saved so what could this be that was pulling her to the altar? She only knew she had to walk down that aisle as the Lord called her, but before she reached the altar, she was slain in the Spirit. (This is an incredible experience where the peace of Almighty God flows throughout your body and your spirit is elevated to heights which man will never attain on earth). She had never experienced anything like this before but when she 'came to,' she was speaking in a language she had never spoken before (speaking in tongues). She asked her mother if she had received the Holy Ghost and she replied, "Aye, Lord, child, all I know is you was speaking in a language I never heard before." Ray finally agreed to go to church with her and got saved there. At that time, Minnie Lee and Steven were the only children they had.

Hattie Lee walked by Mattie Lee Davis' house many times and heard her praying. She was such a fervent woman of God, His anointing affected those around her. When God placed a calling on Hattie Lee to the ministry, her father quickly told her the Bible says the women were to be silent in the church. She prayed hard about this conflict and was led to a scripture that cleared her way: Galatians 3:28 told her we are all one in Jesus, neither male nor female nor Jew nor Greek, so she started her ministry, satisfied she was in His will. She started at the Congregational Holiness Church where Brother Dortch let her preach as she learned the scriptures. The congregation was very supportive and as she got into her message, the amens were

Hattie Lee and Raymond Hill

shouted out… until there was a silent pause. She was relating the story of how Peter denied knowing Jesus three times but she got her facts mixed up and instead of Judas, she continued with 'her version' of the story, saying Peter went out and hung himself. She didn't get any amens for that, but her error was used several times in her future sermons. Ray was her biggest supporter, learning to play the guitar and sing. In 1948, the Hills moved to Miami in search of a better job. Shortly after, Ray and Hattie Lee built the Pentecostal Holiness Church, just north of Miami. Ray was also preaching and pastoring but resigned to build an independent church on the other side of town. They called it the Free Pentecostal Tabernacle. After a few years, the Lord led them to build a new church in Fort Myers, Florida called the Revival Tabernacle. Their son, Steve, was the pastor there for 31 years; then Ray and Hattie Lee returned to Revival Tabernacle for ten years, pastoring until Rev. Hattie Lee (Register) Hill was called to heaven in 1981. All 3 churches are going strong today. The legacy of the covenant made between Hattie Lee Register and the God of her family continues today and for coming generations who choose to serve Him. Here are their 5 children and a few words on the blessings God has given to the family that chose to serve God and teach their generations about His covenant with

Pastor Steve Hill at the Free Pentecostal Tabernacle

them: **KEN HILL** with wife, Winnie, have traveled across the United States evangelizing, and have pastored three churches over the years. Their five children are grown and serve the Lord in various

Ken and Winnie Hill and family

Ken, Steve, Ronald, Minnie Lee Wallin, and Donna Barnhill

Young Pastor Steve and Marilyn Hill

ministries. **STEVEN HILL,** with wife, Marilyn, pastored Free Pentecostal Tabernacle in Hollywood, Florida for 31 years, now in Macclenny, Florida ministering. They have four children and several grandchildren serving the Lord in song ministry. **RONALD HILL,** attends church in Ft. Myers, Florida and sings. He has 3 children. After

Minnie Lee Wallin with Andrew & Anthony

serving in the U.S. Army, he serves in his church however his talents are needed. **MINNIE LEE WALLIN,** and husband, Bill traveled around the United States with the well-known Evangelists A.A. Allen and R.W. Shambach from 1965-1970. The Wallins have three children, Danny, Tracy, and Susan. Anthony

Raymond and Hattie Lee Hill with children

Ambrose, Tracy's son, plays the drums and Andrew, Susan's son, is enjoying Sunday School with his grandparents. Minnie Lee teaches the adult class, plays piano, and sings. She is also co-leader of the Goldtimers senior group that meets seasonally at the First Full Gospel Church in Lake City. **DONNA BARNHILL** attends church in Fort Myers, Florida, was a children's Sunday School teacher, and also sings. She has 2 sons: Rob Edge has pastored his church for years and with his brother Tim Edge, has a music ministry in their church. Only time will tell the lives that have been touched by the Hill family ministry. Three churches were founded. Untold numbers of ministers, singers and musicians spread the gospel, all touched by the seed that was planted in 1946. One young Baptist girl came to revival, got filled with the Holy Ghost and God blessed her family for generations! Holiness is all about Holy Ghost power in action! [Minnie Lee Wallin]

35. STANLEY AND PATRICIA 'PEACHES' ELLIS

This is the testimony of Stanley and 'Peaches' Ellis, concerning her parents (the Albrittons), and her family memorabilia that has been collected through the years: "My family started coming to this church in 1967. My parents, Charles and Barbara Albritton, had five children and we all sat together in the church. (I also remember how the benches in the church kept snagging our good clothes and pinching our legs). The pastor was Ulis Taylor and his wife's name was Luellen. Pastor Ulis Taylor was a very strict pastor. He loved to preach and talk about the eagle. On Sunday mornings, it

Barbara & Charles Albritton

The Albritton Family

Young Peaches & Stan Ellis

seemed like he talked a lot about food. He really enjoyed the 'dinners on the grounds.' Stan Ellis joined the church in 1977 and we were married on June 9th, 1978. Stan served as Assistant Pastor to Brother Taylor as well as Choir Leader and in 1988 he was elected the pastor of First Full Gospel Church and we stayed until mid-1990. We returned in 1993 until now. Our son, Charles, plays guitar, mandolin, piano and drums. Renea, our youngest daughter, is a hair stylist. She sings specials at our church. Our daughter, Michelle and son-in-law, Stephen Jones are Youth Pastors. We are very proud of all our children." The Ellis family is a strong family, built on trust and love. These are the roots of the covenant of God, trust in God and love Him…and each other. It works for all!

Pastor Ulis and Luellen Taylor

Pastor Stan Ellis is a faithful man of God. He takes his calling seriously. He was told by God to go out into the highways and byways and bring in the lost. He does just that. No matter where you see Brother Stan, his life speaks the testimony of his salvation. He is a man of discipline and honor. He was in the Marines where his beliefs were all reinforced: Discipline yourself and be honorable with all men that you may stand before God, unashamed. This is what he would like to share, in the hope someone would be helped: "I would like to tell you about, 'The Greatest Gift of All.' John 3:16-17, says, 'For God so loved the world He gave His only Begotten Son, that whosoever believeth in Him should not perish, but have everlasting life. For

Peaches & Stan Ellis today

God sent not His Son into the world to condemn the world, but that the world through Him might be saved.'

My Friend, God so loved US!! In a world today that is so troubled, so cold and indifferent, so full of hatred and discontent, it is important to know God loves you now! But He not only loves you NOW…He always HAS and He always WILL. His love is the greatest and most powerful force ever known to man. You may think in a world of nuclear weapons, how can this be? These weapons can kill all of humanity and the earth itself. It is true, they can do exactly that. God's love, however, has superceded nuclear power in that He has prevented that by the power of His love. His love is so powerful He changes the heart of man. II Corinthians 5:17 tells us 'Therefore, if any man be in Christ, He is a new creature: old things have passed away; behold, all things are become new."

Charles Ellis

Renea Ellis

"God's love is so powerful it creates new life, a new heart, an opportunity to be changed, forgives and forgets the former things, and develops a life of blessing. He is by far more powerful!!"

"God so loved us that He GAVE! In today's society, it is evident giving is a thing of the past. The Bible tells a story of a man who had so much, he said, 'I will tear down my barns and build new ones; barns large enough to house all my wealth. (Sound familiar?) As a whole, most are wealthy today ~ rich and increased with goods. The Bible again tells us it is more blessed to give than to receive. God's principle teaching is throughout the whole Bible and here on John 3:16, He is the mentor for giving. His example: 'He gave His Son, Jesus,' He died on the cross of Calvary, He was the Supreme sacrifice for humanity. John the Baptist stated 'Behold the Lamb of God, that taketh away the sins of the world.' The question is this: Is this the greatest gift of all? When Jesus went to the cross, God sacrificed His Son, He gave the Best!"

"The greatest gift of all is found within the following resolution: When God so loved us He gave His son, Jesus on the cross, He paid the debt of sin for us and made a way for us to be reconciled to God. The gift that is greatest of all is commonly referred to as SALVATION. All God gave and provided was arranged for us to accept Jesus in our heart as Lord and Savior!"

"By accepting Jesus as Lord, we receive SALVATION for our soul. This is the greatest gift of all!! Romans 10:9-10, 13 tells us how to receive this gift: '...if thou shalt confess with thy mouth the Lord Jesus, and shalt believe in thine heart that God hath raised Him from the dead, thou shalt be saved. For with the heart, man believeth unto righteousness; and with the mouth confession is made unto salvation For whosoever calleth upon the name of the Lord SHALL BE SAVED!!'"

"Pray right now, confess your sin before Him and ask Him to forgive you. Believe on Him and ask Him into your heart. He will save you and pardon you, today."

"Yes, THIS is the greatest gift of all. Your name is now written down in the Lamb's Book of Life!! May the Lord be with you always and God bless you...this is our prayer! First Full Gospel Church." [Pastor Stan Ellis]

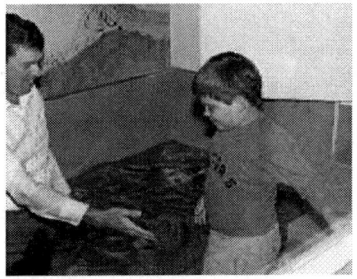

Pastor Ellis Baptizing Stephen Jones

Stephen and Michelle grew up in the First Full Gospel Church. Pastor Stan Ellis, Michelle's father, baptized Stephen when he was just a little boy. Stephen once said to the pastor, "I'm going to marry Michelle!" and he kept that goal in mind until he was standing at the altar, waiting on his lovely bride, Michelle, to say "I do."

Stephen and Michelle Jones are the Youth Pastors at First Full Gospel Church.

36. STEPHEN & MICHELLE JONES

Stephen is also responsible for the Music Ministry of the church. He is a Spirit-filled man of God who is earning his seat of honor among the old time Gospel greats! He has made two anointed Cds, entitled "It Should Have Been Me" and "Pre-Paid Ticket." Stephen is gaining fame as a talented singer and songwriter but he also preaches the Word with compassion and understanding. Michelle is now a free-lance photographer, creating precious memory shots of little children and family groups. We are blessed to have this multi-talented family working together with the First Full Gospel Church. Stephen is employed by Eddie Accardi Chevrolet Mazda in Lake City as Finance Director.

Stephen & Michelle Jones

They have two beautiful children, Kenidy Grace Jones and Jaxon Drew Jones. Stephen once said he could never understand what God meant by 'Unconditional Love,' until he became a father. Now he knows our Heavenly Father doesn't expect us to earn His favor. We could never be 'good enough' to deserve it. It's only by His Grace we learn how much He loves us... unconditionally... when we appear to deserve it the least!

Kenidy Grace and Jaxon Drew Jones

This is his testimony: "I always knew the Lord had a calling on my life. He waited very patiently on me. When I renewed my friendship with Michelle in 1999, I gave my heart away to both the Lord and Michelle. I knew then it was my turn to do something for Him for a change. From the time I first got saved, I could not wait to see what the Lord had in store for me. Shortly after, six of my cousins and I started a singing group called "Forgiven". The Lord opened many doors for that ministry. When the group stopped singing together, I knew the Lord was not finished with me yet, and I would not be satisfied just sitting in a pew somewhere. That is when I started my solo ministry. The Lord has opened up more doors and blessed us more than we could ever have imagined. We are trusting in Him more every day. We don't know just what He has in store for us and our ministry, but we want to be in His will. If He will lead, we will follow." [Stephen Jones]

37. BILLY EARL AND LOUISE SANDERS

When I was tracing the roots of the First Full Gospel Church, I kept asking who played a major role in the progress of the church from the beginning. After a while, the name Billy Earl sounded like an old friend. One after another told how Billy Earl was involved in the building of the church, the gospel music, and eventually he even returned to take center stage at the Watertown reunion. It seems there is no end to the qualifications of a man of God when he lets the spirit lead!

The Sanders are Christians who understand what it means to have a covenant with God. Louise Sanders' father was Alva Boston, an original pastor from years ago. Because they honored that covenant with God, their families have continued to be blessed. This is a picture of the Sanders family:

Center Front: Louise and Billy Earl Sanders surrounded by their children.

The Sanders thank God for being blessed with an incredible gift of music ministry.

This is the testimony given by Billy Earl to explain his family's journey of blessings: "My music career started when I was eight years old. I picked cotton in Red Land, Alabama all summer for my Daddy and on the weekends for a neighbor, Mr. Brooks. I saved my money and ordered a Stella guitar from a Spiegel catalog. All my mother's family played fiddle and guitar. The churches in North Florida loved Mother's singing and music (I guess it runs in the family). I didn't get serious about playing and singing until we moved to Lake City, Florida. I was thirteen when we moved."

"I got married when I was twenty to Louise Boston. Later, I joined the Watertown Congregational Holiness Church. That's where I got my music degree, playing in that church. I started off playing and singing with a good friend, Charles Clyatt. Later, our pastor, Ulis Taylor joined our two man band and we called ourselves, 'The Gospel Travelers.' Later on, we hired two young musicians. Mark Taylor, fifteen years old, played the Dobro and Scott Sanders, eleven years old, played Steel Guitar. They played in The Gospel Travelers Band for a few years until Mark left to join a Bluegrass band called, 'The Bluegrass Prophets.' Scott went to work for the Hinsons out of

Nashville, Tennessee. (I never knew why they quit our band. I guess it must have been the pay). After our two major musicians quit, we settled back down into our home church at Watertown. Later, we formed the 'Southlanders Band,' a great sounding five piece band. We were booked for a year in advance and we decided to move to Nashville, Tennessee. We moved there in 1992, and we have loved Nashville ever since."

"I wrote a song called, 'Home Is Where The Heart Is,' and we want all the people in Lake City, especially Watertown church, to know our hearts lay very close to all of you! We have four sons and two daughters who grew up in Watertown church. Our oldest daughter, Alison, played the organ in that church when she was about fifteen years old. Our youngest daughter played piano in the 'Southlanders Band.'"

"Watertown Church played a very important part in my life. My wife, Louise, was born and raised within sight of Watertown Church. She stood by me for fifty years in this music. She's heard a lot of out-of-tune playing and singing and a lot of loud sound systems in her time."

"The latest song I wrote and recorded was a song I wrote for my wife, Louise, for our fiftieth anniversary, which was on October 10th, 2008. I called it, 'A Diamond In The Sun.' It is a love song about a lady born and raised in Watertown Church. I was the lucky one to come off a cotton farm in Alabama and claim her for my own. Congratulations go to her mother and dad, Alva and Vera Boston, for raising a young lady like her. God bless you all!" Billy E. Sanders

38. CHARLES & BARBARA ALBRITTON

When Peaches Albritton was a little girl, her parents, Charles and Barbara Albritton were praying God would watch over their children and keep them safe and in His will. Charles Albritton has been a member of the First Full Gospel Church for many years, with his wife, Barbara. He is known for being a man of integrity. The Bible has always been his rule book. He has been a hard-working farmer throughout his life and raised his children in the admonition of the Lord. He never would tolerate idleness or being wasteful. He was always devoted to his family but first, he honored God. He knew if he was faithful to the Lord, God would set everything else in proper order.

Barbara Albritton has always been a reserved woman. She knew her husband would make decisions for them. She spent her time loving her children and caring for her home. Barbara always was a beautiful woman, being very selective about her hair, clothing and appearance, but her greatest beauty was always her spirit. It is no secret Barbara is personally acquainted with her Savior. She spent many hours over the years in tearful prayers for the

The Albritton Children

Lord to move on behalf of one of her children. He has never let her down. God has seen her through many trials and hardships, and each time she rises from the ashes a more powerful woman of God. Several children still remember her as their school bus driver. She retired from driving recently, but those children will always have a very special place in her heart. She enjoyed the time she spent with them. Recently, Sister Barbara was very ill and spent several months in and out of the hospital, at times, standing at death's door. Her husband sat by her side. The family kept praying God would heal her and the congregation also fasted and prayed for her condition to improve. As usual, God came right on time to restore His daughter that He may receive the praise and glory. Brother Albritton told us God had a reason they went through those trials. He proved He was still God!

Charles Albritton has been walking with God for many years, and he knows the sound of His voice. He would be the first to tell you God doesn't need to speak in man's voice to make you listen. Sometimes, God speaks directly to your heart through His Word. Sometimes, He shows you a portion of the Sunday School lesson to ponder. Then there are the times, when God uses your own common sense to tell you to do the right thing. Life is a series of lessons, and the education we get through life experiences are precious gifts. God expects you to use the wisdom you have learned over the years, and Charles has put it to good use. He still advises his children, and even his grandchildren, to take it all to the Lord and hear what 'thus saith the Lord;' but then it's up to you to put it into action, and you better do it, too. Brother Albritton will be quick to tell you, if you don't listen to God, you better believe, you'll be sorry and wish everything was right between you and God. You can't make it to heaven on a wish bone. You got to get a little backbone and get to work trying to help yourself. Hard work will make you strong, and obedience will get you to heaven.   [Charles & Barbara Albritton]

39. HEATHER REGISTER

Heather Register

Heather is a willing vessel for God. She humbly pleads with the lost to seek salvation. This is her testimony: "I began serving the Lord in 1998, and His mercy and goodness are beyond imagination! Somehow along the way, I got discouraged, as people often do. I fell into sin, and backslid. It wasn't an easy road - I was addicted to drugs, nicotine and became involved with alcohol. I had a lifestyle that wasn't pleasing to God or me. I was depressed to say the least! The devil made me feel it was impossible to receive forgiveness and salvation for my sins, but God is so full of compassion and mercy that I came to church one Sunday morning and gave my heart and life back to Him. It was by far the best choice I've ever made. God gave me a new beginning and I'm so grateful! My desire is to be all I can be in Him and to be in service for Him! He is my everything and no matter what I go through, God is there! He is my help, my Healer, my Deliverer, and my Strength! Though Satan tries to tell me God doesn't hear my prayers and God can't do what I ask, I must remember - SATAN IS A LIAR! I have learned to be encouraged, not discouraged. God has brought me so far! He's filled me with the Holy Ghost! He never ceases to bring love, peace and joy to my life! I know without a doubt God can do anything! Luke 1:37 says, 'For with God nothing shall be impossible." [Heather Register]

40. BILL BALLANCE

He's a quiet man who keeps to himself. He sees someone in need, he reaches deep into his pockets and gives without hesitation.

As Sister Joyce Brown says, "He's a good man and he has a good heart." When the musicians take their places, Bill plays his tambourine with them. It's a small contribution to the music ministry, but when Bill's chair is empty, he is greatly missed. I asked him, "If you gave advice to make a difference in someone's life, what would it be?" He replied, "Stay in the Word. Read it. Study it. Pray over it and then live it." That's pretty good advice from a man who's just eighty-one years 'young'. [Bill Ballance]

Bill Ballance

41. ZELMER MAE ELLIS

She was nine years of age when she got saved. Mama and Papa were sure proud. Her parents were Christians of the Pentecostal faith. But they were also migrant farm workers. Mama was a quiet woman and Papa was strict in his Biblical beliefs. It was that strong faith that healed a three year old and her father of typhoid fever. She married Wilson Ellis and had three sons and a daughter. One son, Stanley became a preacher and escorted his father to the altar when he got saved.   [Zelmer Mae Ellis]

Zelmer Mae Ellis

42. DAVID AND ANN COLLINS

David is a man who trusts God completely. He turned to God when he was out of work. That's not a good place to be when your family is counting on you. He turned it all over to God and continued searching for a job. He knew God would answer his prayer, but he also knew that God didn't want him to stop looking while waiting on God. A couple of weeks passed and one night David came into the church grinning. God had not only found him a job, but now he was turning away companies that wanted to hire him. That kind of faith moves mountains!

Ann Collins is the sweetest person you'll find. We call her the 'card lady.' If you have a birthday, anniversary, or she just feels like you need it, there will be a bright card in the mail with lots of faith lifting stickers attached! She has a spirit of love. The only time Ann appears to be the least 'ruffled' is if she has forgotten to send a special card with a personal message inside from 'David and Ann Collins,' with love.

Davis and Ann continue to pray for their children. They aren't the only parents out there praying for your children's salvation!

Ann & David Collins

But remember this: They learned to walk and talk by watching Mommy and Daddy. So keep on being a good Christian. Your children are still watching! Let them observe you reading God's Word and calling their names out to the Lord. Let them see the joy from the Lord that replaces the stresses of life. Someday, they'll seek what it is that you have makes you feel so good!

43. AMANDA MANSKE

She started coming to church with her Grandmother Betty and she soaked up all the Spirit she could get. She needed to stock up because she was battling a lot of hard times at home and in her life, but she's one determined single Mom, and I'm believing she's not only going to make it but she's going to bring others in to meet the Lord. This is her testimony: "My name is Amanda Manske. I am twenty-six years old. I grew up with an alcoholic mother and no father at all. Church wasn't an issue when I was young. I began smoking when I was about thirteen. My mom drank so I figured I could do it too. Then the drinking led on to drugs, always looking for a greater high. I did graduate from high school despite the turmoil in my life. After my graduation, I tried every drug I could get my

Amanda Manske & baby Gracie

hands on. I figured something would fill the void I had in my life."

"When I was nineteen I joined the army, but I know now I was trying to run from the problems in my life. While I was in Basic Training, I started going to church and really enjoyed it. In hindsight, I believe the Lord was feeding me spiritual food to sustain me in the months ahead, for I was sent to Iraq for the first six months of the war."

"Being in a war zone with bullets flying all around you and bombs exploding night and day, I took comfort from those services I attended during Basic Training. On the third of September, my convoy was cut off by a staff car. My driver lost control of the truck, and flipped the vehicle over, but an amazing thing happened to me... just as we started to roll over, 'someone' grabbed the back of my flak vest and pulled me back into the truck. I could have been killed if the truck had rolled on me, but the Lord saved my life. There was no one else around me so I knew it had to be the hand of God. I wasn't saved spiritually but I remembered Grandma telling me how Jesus protects and saves. He loved me even then, when I wasn't giving Him any of my love."

"I was medically evacuated stateside after a week in Germany, and despite my miracle from God, I started drinking again quite a bit. Soon I got hooked on a hard drug ~ methamphetamine, a drug I believe was the devil himself. My life started falling apart but it didn't happen all at once. I prided myself foolishly that I only did meth on weekends. I thought I was strong enough to handle it. I had accomplished quite a bit! I had rented an apartment, furnished it nicely, saved some money...not to mention I survived a war! The Army counselors became aware I was on drugs and ordered me to rehab or I'd lose my G.I. benefits. I wasn't as much in control as I thought. I stayed off drugs for about three months but that demon drug came back to get me and soon I lost everything for which I had worked. The only thing I had left in my life was my dog and my car in which I had to live. The army released me with a 90% disability and honorably discharged me. The drugs were controlling me by then and soon I was arrested."

"I wanted to come back to Florida in hopes of putting some order to my life, but before I got past Mobile, Alabama I wrecked my car and totaled the only possession I had left. My sister came to rescue me but all I wanted to do was go back to Colorado with my old friends and get high. This time the mountains of Colorado had more to offer me."

"My friends were there; the drugs were there, but I realized my desires for that life weren't there any more. I went high into the mountains and talked to God. I cried out to Him like an abandoned child and He heard me. He had never been far from me; I was the one who pulled away from Him. Since that day in the mountains when I asked Jesus into my heart, I have not had any withdrawal symptoms and I never craved the drugs any more. The Lord once again saved my life. In October, I realized I was going to have a baby. The doctors told me I wouldn't be able to carry her full-term, but He gave me a beautiful, healthy baby girl. Before this, I never thanked God for the intervention He had done for me, and each time, I returned to the demons of my past. Now I am thankful for all His blessings, my salvation, and for giving me a new life. I know from where my strength comes and with it He sends perfect peace. I am now in my second year of college, majoring in psychology, with hopes of making a difference in the lives of drug addicts. My life is blessed. To God be the glory!" [Amanda Manske]

44. EARL AND PANSY GREEN

The Watertown Congregational Holiness Church was known for the strong faith of the families. They didn't just 'come to church.' They WERE the church. They really practiced the beliefs that were preached and their children were raised by the book…the Bible! The Greens were one of the those families. Did it really do any good to be so strict with the children back then? Did it make any difference in the lives of these children? Where are

Earl & Pansy Green with Earl, Jr. & Juanna

they now? Pastor Ulis Taylor officiated at Juanna Green's wedding to Mike Duncan in The Watertown Church, April 13th, 1980. Her parents, Rev. Earl and Pansy Green are to the left of the bride.

Some may disagree with the 'spare the rod and spoil the child' wisdom of the scriptures, but God didn't make it an option. He knew

Mike & Juanna 'Green' Duncan

ALL His children needed to learn obedience, and it needed to start in the home. The Greens were workers in the Church. Brother Green, at times, served as interim pastor. There were plenty of church dinners on the grounds, but the most memorable times the 'children' remember were the revivals that lasted late into the night, and no one tried to sneak out. There was too much going on, and no one wanted to miss any of the excitement from the Holy Ghost. Lives were changed and children were formed into men and women who knew all about the covenant made with father Abraham that would include his seed. That promise carried down to us; if we would be His people, He would be our God and bless our families for generations.

Earl Green, Sr. and Pansy Green lived their lives under the covenant, and their children reaped the rewards. They are carrying on the Christian faith in their families. Earl Green, Jr. watched his dad sing tenor in a group called 'The Gospel Travelers' with Billy Sanders, Charles Clyatt and Ulis Taylor. (Remember this: Children learn by what they see!) Earl started to play guitar and sing, 'just like Dad.' In 1976, he started traveling with 'The Gospelites.' Then he started a group called 'The New Horizons.'

Mercy Mountain Boys
Donnie, Mitch & Earl

He joined 'The Singing Reps' as lead singer around 1982. Earl had great success when he sang with 'Highway 7.' In Watertown, we're partial to a song he wrote and sang , called 'The Old- Fashioned Way,' a song about our old church by the railroad tracks. We're honored to remember the Green's legacy, a covenant honored!

45. ULIS AND LUELLEN TAYLOR

Pastor Ulis and Sister Luellen Taylor are close friends with the congregation at the First Full Gospel Chuch as well as New Beginnings

where he pastors. Their love for God and
His people is what makes them so special.
They are daily in the Word and and their
life is the epitome of what God's blessings
can do when you are faithful. Brother
Taylor studies the Word and seeks divine
guidance and understanding for each verse.
He is an excellent teacher and mentor, for

Pastor Ulis and Luellen Taylor

he desires to be like Jesus. What better example could any of
us follow? This is Ulis Taylor's testimony: "I started pastoring
the First Full Gospel Church when it was in the Congregational
Holiness movement. We came out of Congregational Holiness
in 1970. We took on the name of the First Full Gospel Church,
which was my idea and the congregation approved of it."

"I guess the highlight of my pastoring the church was the
building of the present day sanctuary. In 1968, we had a great
revival with Rev. Lowell Haynes and twenty-five people got saved
and some received the Holy Ghost baptism! Some of our revivals
were preached by evangelists like Rev. Hubert Hammond, Randy
Hobbs, Lloyd Morgan, and Lowell Haynes."

"The present pastor of First Full Gospel is Brother Stan Ellis,
and I can remember when he got saved. It was on a Sunday
evening before the service even got started. It was my privilege
to lead him to the Lord. I would like to mention in closing that we
had the best Sunday School attendance in 1969 and the number
was 167."

"We have had some great services with miracles, healings
and the most of all souls were saved. When they were trying

Glenda Richardson

to raise the funds to build the new sanctuary,
one young woman took it as a special project to
raise as much as she could for the church. Glenda
Williams Richardson was loved by all who knew
her. She died very young, and though she is gone
from us now, we look forward to seeing her on the
other side with her crown. Too often we say too
little to those we love most. We were blessed when
all our friends and our family came to First Full Gospel to celebrate
our anniversary. This is one of our best-loved pictures which we will

both treasure forever, our four sons with Mom and Dad. [Ulis Taylor]

46. CHARLES AND JANICE CLYATT

Rev. Ulis and Sis. Luellen Taylor surrounded by sons

Charles and Janice Clyatt have been around Watertown Church for many years. When the music starts and the Spirit is moving, one thing is certain; Janice is right up front

Janice & Charles Clyatt

near the altar, breathing in the breath of God as the anointing fills the house. As for Charles, he probably was the one who picked up his guitar first to invite the congregation to start praising the Lord. Don't ask how long he's played bluegrass because he really IS bluegrass. He has mastered the music that has been stirring hearts for generations!

47. MARVIN & JUNE WILLIAMS

Marvin Williams is the Sunday School Superintendent for the First Full Gospel Church. He fulfills his duties well and has for many years. He treasures those Sunday School lessons and gains a lot of spiritual strength from them. We could all use more spiritual strength. Sister June is so quiet and shy

June & Marvin Williams

but you can see her eyes sparkle when you mention her Lord and Marvin. They are all three best friends.

CHAPTER XIX

I Cried, "Lord!" And He Said, "I Am With You Always!"

Father, You have given me a calling in my life, and I am humbled by the privilege. I didn't know how to love until You showed me how much You love me…I never knew how to forgive until You forgave me. I didn't feel prized until I found out the price You paid for me. I never saw beauty until You showed me the glory of Your world. I had no hope until You showed me unlimited possibilities. You took a broken child who wasn't needed and taught her to be a woman highly favored. You took a man who gave up on being loved and showed him Your love and mercy. You brought them together to walk in Your pathways. Together, they learned to lean on You and each other. Two misfits in neglect came together. Two broken vessels, without a prayer, learned

Helen & Danny Hill

how to pray. Past mistakes were erased and a three-fold cord was woven, for strength, never to be broken again. No one thought we would ever amount to anything. He stayed drunk and never allowed himself to fall deeply in love with a woman. They always came, like storms in his life, leaving paths of total destruction. It's what he expected, and they never let him down. He offered them little hope of a lasting relationship. He didn't even know if there was such a thing. So when the fighting started, he hid in a bottle while the storm left behind a spiraling cascade of destruction in his life, taking away children, and any hope of having them back in his life. He was damaged goods and his children inherited the empty hopelessness of both unmarried parents. He didn't try for a better life; someone would just take it away from him, and I was too blinded by my pain to see hope for myself.

But then one night, when we were exhausted from fighting to survive, You just reached out You hand and said, "It's okay now. I've got you," and our fall was broken! You picked us up, dusted us off and sent angels to minister to us... Angels like Marshall and Linda Davis; Janice Davis who cared enough to show her concern when I got too tired after cancer; the Johnson family who counseled and prayed for us as friends. They brought us to the Carolina mountains to enjoy the retreat for a week. Who would have thought a little girl from the bad side of town, with no friends, would end up with loving ANGELS for friends?! God, You did that! You prepared a husband for me. You cleaned him up and took away the hindrances in his life. You picked me up and showed me I could love someone without being afraid. Then you surrounded us with Christians, real friends like the Wallins, the Ellis', the Davises...(and that's a bunch of Davises), the Widneys, the Millers, Martinez...I could go on and on! We are so blessed!! And You did this miracle! You created a new life for us. You gave us a home, and a truck (and a real Christian car dealer with a family for me to love and spoil), YOU did it ALL! You gave us miracles and blessings for which we didn't even know we could ask! How wonderful You are! Amazing and awesome is my Lord...I thank You for the privilege of recording all the testimonies we received. At first I was curious about Your plan, but now I see! Everyone who had a testimony received an answer from God. Yet each one was unique! You answered every need for everyone! I could see their strengths, but I saw no failures. I was looking through God-colored glasses! I was using my spiritual vision and I saw the children You love so dearly and the qualities they have that make them so special to You! Now their testimonies will be sent into the highways and byways and many lost shall come to You for answers. Thank You, Lord!

I still need to know...for years I've searched for that spiritual fountain where the seed of faith begins, but I'm still wandering... and wondering! Where is the root of Your HOLY GROUND? Lord, have I missed it?

And a still small voice from heaven said, "My child...you are My Holy Ground. You always had the key to heavenly places, even before you were born. For I kept them in the palm of My hand; you had but to reach out to Me and I would open all doors unto you. Do you not see you have been reaching for Me throughout your quest?

For now I say to you, 'Ask and it shall be given you; seek, and ye shall find; knock and it shall be opened unto you.' You are my children. I come to give you life and love in abundance, and to your children and generations to come, for I am the Lord thy God." And today, you and I are standing on Holy Ground…a place where God waits for you… to make a covenant with you. He wants to be your Father, the King of Kings and Almighty God. In return, He gives you a new birth… a new beginning, with Jesus. Close the door on yesterday, and seek the kingdom of God and all your needs will be supplied.

CHAPTER XX

I Trust My Lord ~ For He Gives Me Abundant Life

First Full Gospel Church

Lake City [Watertown], Florida   November, 2008

Once I was a child, alone in my search for Holy Ground, but He led me to the Living Waters, and I never thirst. He fed me on the Bread of Life and I never hunger. I became a member of the body of Christ. Together, in unity, we praise His Holy Name! "For where two or three are gathered together in My name, there am I in the midst of them," says our Lord, and the Holy Ghost moves on our Holy Ground!